Low Fat
MEXICAN RECIPES

by

Shayne and Lee Fischer

GOLDEN WEST ☼ PUBLISHERS

Front cover photo © 1997 Lois Ellen Frank/Westlight

Library of Congress Cataloging-in-Publication Data
Fischer, Shayne
   Low Fat Mexican Recipes / by Shayne and Lee Fischer
      p.   cm.
   Includes glossaries and index.
   ISBN 1-885590-12-1
   1. Cookery, Mexican.   2. Low Fat diet—Recipes   I. Fischer, Lee
   II. Title
TX716.M4F56   1997   97-46337
   641.5'638—dc21   CIP

Printed in the United States of America

Information in this book is deemed to be authentic and accurate by authors and publisher. However, they disclaim any liability incurred in connection with the use of information appearing in this book.

Golden West Publishers, Inc.
4113 N. Longview Ave.
Phoenix, AZ 85014, USA
(602) 265-4392

Table of Contents

Introduction 4

Glossary 6

Appetizers 7

Breakfasts 21

Soups & Salads 27

Side Dishes 41

Main Dishes 53

Desserts 77

Beverages 83

Chile Glossary 89

Index 90

About the Authors 94

Introduction

We grew up in the Southwest where Mexican food is a way of life. Traditional Mexican food is fairly high in fat. Rich sauces, lots of cheese, tortillas and chips that are fried. Since we eat a lot of Mexican food and we want to stay healthy and active it became important to develop a way of eating our favorite Mexican foods with as little fat intake as possible. This book represents the culmination of our adaptation and experimentation; a book of traditional Mexican recipes that have flavor with much less fat. In some recipes we have eliminated fat altogether. In others the fat content is dramatically lowered.

For a healthy diet, nutritionists recommend that fat intake should represent no more than 30% of your daily calories. Proteins and carbohydrates contain 4 calories per gram while fat has 9 calories per gram. So a reasonable fat gram intake for someone on an 1800-calorie daily diet might be 540 calories, or, 60 grams, from fat, at a maximum. We have provided the fat gram content on a per serving basis for each recipe. In some instances we indicate zero grams. A negligible amount of fat may exist in the recipes, but the amount is so insignificant that we rounded down to zero. Recipes which include meat will have the highest amounts of fat. Remember to always buy the leanest cuts that you can, remove all visible fats and skins, and cook the meats until well done, as the longer cooking time allows for more fat to melt out. Be sure to drain meats thoroughly so all fats that have oozed out can be disposed of.

As all oils do contain fat we have limited the amount of oils utilized. The highest levels of saturated fat are in animal fats, while vegetable fats are usually lower. However, certain oils such as coconut and palm oils, are highly saturated and should be used sparingly. There are many good books on the market today that can provide valuable information regarding saturated and unsaturated fats and appropriate consumption.

This cookbook presents healthful and tasty alternatives to fried foods. We include methods for creating your own baked

tortilla chips and taco and tostada shells. Throughout the book, the analyses are for these baked alternatives. Also, most stores now offer a variety of baked chips.

As food manufacturers have responded to consumers' demands for healthier foods, the list of available low-fat foods continues to grow. While most corn tortillas have a minimal amount of fat (less than 1 gram per tortilla) there are corn tortillas on the market with virtually no fat, which are the ones we use for determining the fat gram analyses. Low-fat and fat free cheeses are now widely available in our supermarkets and natural foods stores. In our cooking and baking tests we worked with several different types of cheeses and with different fat percentages. Our best results were with cheeses that had a 50% lower fat content. We found that the cheeses that had a higher no-fat rating did not perform well in kitchen tests, i.e., not melting, rubbery texture and a flawed taste. In our recipes, when low fat cheese is listed, we are referring to the 50% variety.

Many recipes call for a variety of canned beans. You can now purchase fat free canned beans at the grocery store. Again, we are making the assumption that fat free canned beans are utilized in the recipes, unless only a low fat variety is available (some of the beans have an inherent amount of fat naturally). Remember that lard free is not the same thing as fat free, so be sure to read package labels to determine what you are really buying.

Knowing that the flavor in many foods does come from fat, it is a blessing there are so many spices and spicy additions to Mexican food. Spices such as cumin and oregano, herbs like cilantro and chiles in a dazzling array of sizes, colors and flavors help to provide Mexican dishes with their distinctive flavors.

Thank you for purchasing this cookbook. Chances are you are buying this for yourself, your family or friends. We want to congratulate you on your decision to explore the tasty, healthy alternatives presented in *Low Fat Mexican Recipes*.

Shayne & Lee Fischer

Glossary

Arroz: Rice

Burro/Burrito: Flour tortillas filled with a mixture of choice, folded and rolled and frequently topped with a variety of salsas.

Café: Coffee

Camarones: Shrimp

Chiles: See Chile Glossary page 89

Chiles Rellenos: Cheese-stuffed peppers, battered and fried.

Cilantro: Also known as Chinese Parsley. Cilantro is the leaf of the Coriander plant. The leaves, which can be used fresh or dried, impart a distinctive, almost "soapy" flavor.

Cumin: A key spice in many Mexican foods, cumin is also used in many Indian dishes, particularly curry mixtures.

Enchiladas: Rolled corn tortillas filled with cheese, chicken, meat, seafood or vegetables, topped with melted cheese and a green or red chile sauce.

Ensalada: Salad

Fajitas: Marinated beef (originally skirt steak) or chicken strips, cooked or grilled, served on a sizzling platter with grilled vegetables. Typically piled onto warm flour tortillas, rolled up and eaten by hand.

Flan: A caramel custard dessert.

Frijoles: Beans

Frijoles Refritos: Refried beans

Guacamole: An avocado mixture that can be served as an appetizer with dips, or as an accompaniment to main dishes, or as a main ingredients, as in *Guacamole Tostadas.*

Huevo: Egg

Huevos Rancheros: Mexican country-style eggs.

Jicama (hee-cah-mah): A tuber resembling a large, brown potato, similar in texture and taste to a water chestnut.

Masa Harina: Corn flour

Menudo: A tasty mixture of beef tripe (which has been cubed, seasoned and boiled until tender), hominy and seasonings.

Nachos: Tortilla chips topped with a variety of ingredients, usually served as an appetizer.

Papas: Potatoes

Picante: Hot, as in spicy foods.

Pollo: Chicken

Quesadilla: A crisped corn or flour tortilla folded over with cheese and other ingredients inside.

Queso: Cheese

Salsa Verde: A green sauce made with tomatillos.

Taco: A tortilla, usually corn, that is folded in half, baked or fried, and filled with a variety of ingredients. Soft tacos are made with heated corn or flour tortillas.

Tomatillo: A small, firm green tomato-like fruit which is covered with a papery husk. Used in *Salsa Verde.*

Tortillas: A thin pancake-like "bread" which can be made of flour or corn. Tortillas are utilized in countless Mexican dishes.

Tostada: A corn tortilla, served flat and crisped (baked or fried), layered with refried beans, ground beef, lettuce, tomatoes, etc.

Appetizers

Low Fat Corn Tortilla Chips 8

Low Fat Flour Tortilla Chips 8

Basic Salsa 9

Fiery Salsa 9

Quick Salsa 10

Cilantro Salsa 10

Salsa Verde (Green Salsa) 11

Salsa Picante (Hot Salsa) 11

Creamy Pinto Bean Dip 12

Black Bean Dip 12

Chunky Bean Dip 13

Chef's Choice Bean Dip 13

Spicy Jicama Sticks 14

Pickled Potatoes 14

Spicy Medley 15

Stuffed Green Chiles 15

Tuna-stuffed Jalapeños 16

Tortilla Roll-ups 16

Corn Crisps 17

Veggie Quesadillas 17

Avocado Dip 18

Salsa Blanca 18

Nachos 19

Pico de Gallo 19

Baked Fiesta Dip 20

Layered Dip 20

Chips

What could be more of a traditional Mexican food appetizer than salsa and chips? Whether you're entertaining or dining alone you'll love the taste of these chips and enjoy the guilt-free satisfaction of knowing you're snacking the low-fat way. Unlike restaurant or many commercial chips these chips are baked, not fried, thereby eliminating fat-laden oils.

Low Fat Corn Tortilla Chips

12 CORN TORTILLAS

Preheat oven to 400°. Stack tortillas three-at-a-time and cut into wedge shapes. Arrange in single layer on cookie sheet. Bake on top rack of oven for approximately three minutes or until crisp. To avoid overbaking, check frequently and remove from oven at first signs of browning.

Savory suggestion: For spicy Mexican-flavored chips, slightly moisten tortillas, before baking, and season with garlic salt, chili powder and ground cayenne pepper.

Each corn tortilla contains 0 fat grams.

Low Fat Flour Tortilla Chips

10 (7- inch) FLOUR TORTILLAS

Preheat oven to 400°. Stack tortillas five-at-a-time and cut into wedge shapes. Arrange in single layer on cookie sheet. Bake on top rack of oven for approximately two minutes or until crisp. To avoid overbaking, check frequently and remove from oven after initial browning. Serve warm.

Savory suggestion: Using spray bottle, slightly moisten unbaked tortillas with water and sprinkle with salt, garlic powder and chili powder.

Each flour tortilla contains 2 fat grams.

Salsas

What would Mexican food be without salsa? Salsa is Spanish for sauce and there are literally hundreds of different types of salsas. Salsas can be used as a dip for appetizers or as an accompaniment for main and side dishes.

Basic Salsa

4 med. TOMATOES, finely chopped
1 can (8 oz.) TOMATO SAUCE
1 can (4 oz.) diced GREEN CHILES, drained
3 GREEN ONIONS, chopped
1 clove GARLIC, crushed
1/4 tsp. OREGANO
1/4 tsp. ground CUMIN
1/4 tsp. CHILI POWDER
SALT and PEPPER to taste

Combine all ingredients in glass bowl. Cover and refrigerate. For best results make the day before.

Makes 3 cups.   Fat grams per serving = 0

Fiery Salsa

2 lg. TOMATOES, diced
1 can (8 oz.) TOMATO SAUCE
1/2 tsp. GARLIC SALT
1/2 tsp. OREGANO
1 tsp. CHILI POWDER
2 JALAPEÑO PEPPERS, seeded and diced
1 can (4 oz.) diced GREEN CHILES, drained

Combine all ingredients in glass bowl. Cover and refrigerate overnight.

Makes approximately 2 cups.   Fat grams per serving = 0

Quick Salsa

1 can (15 oz.) STEWED TOMATOES, crushed
1 can (8 oz.) TOMATO SAUCE
1 can (7 oz.) GREEN CHILES, diced
1 sm. ONION, diced
1/2 tsp. GARLIC SALT
1/2 tsp. SUGAR
1/4 tsp. CAYENNE

Combine all ingredients and chill for several hours before serving.

Makes 4 cups.   Fat grams per serving = 0

Cilantro Salsa

1 can (15 oz.) ITALIAN PLUM TOMATOES, drained, chopped
1 can (8 oz.) TOMATO SAUCE
1/4 cup fresh CILANTRO, finely chopped
1 can (4 oz.) diced GREEN CHILES, drained
1/2 tsp. ground CUMIN
1/2 tsp. GARLIC SALT
1/4 tsp. ONION SALT
PEPPER to taste

Combine all ingredients and chill for several hours before serving.

Makes 4 cups.   Fat grams per serving = 0

Salsa Verde
(Green Salsa)

6 ANAHEIM CHILES, roasted, seeded and diced
1/2 cup fresh CILANTRO, chopped
1 sm. ONION, chopped
1 clove GARLIC, pressed
1/2 tsp. ground CUMIN
1 Tbsp. LEMON JUICE
SALT and PEPPER to taste

Place all ingredients in blender and blend until desired thickness. Refrigerate for several hours.

Makes 2 cups. Fat grams per serving = 0

Salsa Picante
(Hot Salsa)

Watch out, this is really HOT!

3 med. TOMATOES, chopped
1 GREEN BELL PEPPER, seeded and chopped
1 med. ONION, chopped
1 crushed CHILTEPIN
2 sm. YELLOW CHILES, seeded and diced
1/2 tsp. GARLIC SALT
1 Tbsp. LIME or LEMON JUICE
4 Tbsp. chopped fresh CILANTRO

Combine all ingredients and let chill.

Makes 2 cups. Fat grams per serving = 0

Bean Dips

Creamy Pinto Bean Dip

This wholesome, low fat dip can be served heated or chilled.

1 can (15 oz.) whole PINTO BEANS, drained
1 pkg. (8 oz.) FAT FREE CREAM CHEESE, room temperature
4 Tbsp. SALSA
1/2 tsp. GARLIC SALT

Combine all ingredients in a food processor and blend to desired consistency. Serve with tortilla chips or spread on baked corn tortillas that have been quartered (these can be heated in toaster oven or microwave.)

Fat grams per serving = <1

Black Bean Dip

Ounce for ounce black beans are highest in protein. These smoky-tasting beans lend themselves to salsas, dips, salads and much more.

1 can (15 oz.) FAT FREE BLACK BEANS, with juice
2 cloves GARLIC
1 Tbsp. LEMON JUICE
1/2 tsp. SALT
2 Tbsp. SALSA

In a food processor or blender, purée all ingredients together. Serve with low fat tortilla chips, crackers or wedges of pita bread.

Fat grams per serving = <1

Chunky Bean Dip

This dip is delicious when served with vegetables, chips or lahvosh.

1 cup whole, cooked, mashed PINTO BEANS
1 stalk CELERY, chopped
2 Tbsp. FAT FREE MAYONNAISE
1/2 tsp. GARLIC SALT

Combine all ingredients together and mix well. Refrigerate before serving.

Fat grams per serving = <1

Chef's Choice Bean Dip

This recipe can be made with your favorite whole beans. It will be so tasty you may want to serve it as a side dish.

1 can (15 oz.) FAT FREE BEANS (choice of PINTO, KIDNEY,
    BLACK, GARBANZO, NAVY), drained and rinsed
2 lg. TOMATOES, diced
1/4 cup diced ONIONS
1 CUCUMBER, peeled and diced
1 can (4 oz.) chopped GREEN CHILES
1/2 cup chopped fresh CILANTRO
1/4 tsp. GARLIC SALT
1 Tbsp. LEMON JUICE

Combine all ingredients in a glass bowl and refrigerate for at least one hour. Serve chilled.

Fat grams per serving = <1

Spicy Jicama Sticks

Jicama (HEE-kah-mah) is often referred to as the Mexican potato. Its water chestnut-type texture and taste is delicious both raw and cooked. A good source of vitamin C and potassium, it can be found in most supermarkets and in Mexican markets. Try these tasty snacks in place of tortilla chips.

1 med. JICAMA
GARLIC SALT
CHILI POWDER
CAYENNE

Wash and peel jicama. Cut into sticks or chips and rinse in cold water. Drain and sprinkle lightly with seasonings, using cayenne sparingly. These make great and unusual appetizers for your relish tray.

Fat grams per serving = 0

Pickled Potatoes

1 can (15 oz.) WHOLE WHITE SMALL POTATOES
2 Tbsp. VINEGAR
2 GREEN ONIONS, chopped
1 can (4 oz.) diced JALAPEÑOS
SALT and PEPPER to taste

Drain potatoes and place in glass bowl. Add vinegar, onion and jalapeños. Season with salt and pepper. Cover and refrigerate. Allow potatoes to marinate overnight. Serve chilled.

Fat grams per serving = 0

Spicy Medley

1 med. JICAMA, peeled and diced in 1/2-inch chunks
1 can (15 oz.) WHOLE WHITE SMALL POTATOES
8 oz. BABY CARROTS, fresh or frozen
2 cups CAULIFLOWER FLORETS, parboiled
1 med. ONION, sliced
1 can (4 oz.) diced JALAPEÑOS
1/4 cup VINEGAR
2 Tbsp. LEMON JUICE
1/2 tsp. SUGAR
1/2 tsp. GARLIC SALT
1/4 tsp. PEPPER

In a large mixing bowl combine all ingredients. Mix thoroughly so vegetables are coated with marinade. Refrigerate overnight. Before serving, toss vegetables lightly to redistribute marinade.

Fat grams per serving = 0

Stuffed Green Chiles

2 cans (4 oz. each) WHOLE GREEN CHILES or use
    fresh if available
4 oz. FAT FREE CREAM CHEESE
1 GREEN ONION, finely chopped
SALT to taste

Drain chiles, slice lengthwise and place on a platter. Combine cream cheese, onion and salt and mix thoroughly. Spread cream cheese mixture into chiles and cover and refrigerate until ready to serve.

Fat grams per serving = 0

Tuna-stuffed Jalapeños

A unique taste treat that will be a hit at your next party. The tuna helps to mellow the heat from the jalapeños, but beware, some jalapeños are hotter than others!

12 whole PICKLED JALAPEÑOS
1 can (6 oz.) water-packed TUNA
1-2 Tbsp. FAT FREE MAYONNAISE
1 tsp. LEMON JUICE
SALT and PEPPER to taste
PAPRIKA

Split and halve jalapeños and carefully remove seeds and stems. Place in a single layer on serving platter. In a small bowl mix drained tuna, mayonnaise, lemon juice, salt and pepper. Mixture should be stiff. Spoon tuna into jalapeño halves. Sprinkle with paprika. Cover with plastic wrap and refrigerate until ready to serve.

Fat grams per serving = 0

Tortilla Roll-ups

1 pkg. (8 oz.) FAT FREE CREAM CHEESE
2 Tbsp. FAT FREE SOUR CREAM
1 GREEN ONION, finely minced
1 can (4 oz.) GREEN CHILES, diced
1/4 tsp. GARLIC SALT
6 (10-inch) FLOUR TORTILLAS

Blend together all ingredients except flour tortillas. Spread mixture evenly over each tortilla. Roll tortillas tightly. Cover and chill thoroughly. Slice each roll-up into half-inch slices.

Fat grams per serving = <1

Corn Crisps

6 CORN TORTILLAS
1/2 cup shredded LOW FAT CHEDDAR CHEESE
3 Tbsp. diced GREEN CHILES
1 TOMATO, diced

Preheat oven to 400°. Place tortillas on cookie sheet and sprinkle each tortilla with grated cheese and chiles. Bake for two minutes, or until cheese bubbles. Remove to serving platter(s) and sprinkle with diced tomato. Serve with **SALSA** and **FAT FREE SOUR CREAM.**

Serves 6.   Fat grams per serving = 1.5

Veggie Quesadillas

These delightful appetizers can be baked in the oven or heated to a crisp on the stove, in a frying pan or hot griddle.

4 (10-inch) FLOUR TORTILLAS
1/2 cup shredded LOW FAT CHEDDAR CHEESE
1 can (4 oz.) diced GREEN CHILES, drained
1 sm. ONION, finely chopped
1 TOMATO, diced

If baking in the oven, preheat to 350°. Place tortillas on cookie sheet. Top with cheese, chiles, onion and tomato. Bake for two minutes, fold in half, and continue baking until crisp, approximately three more minutes. Remove to serving platter. For faster and crispier results, use the broiler method: place loaded tortillas (still on cookie sheet) under broiler. As soon as cheese starts to melt, fold tortillas and broil until crisp (watch carefully as cooking time will be greatly reduced.)   Cut into wedges and serve with **SALSA.**

Serves 8.   Fat grams per serving = 1.1

Avocado Dip

While avocados are not exactly low in fat, they just taste so darn good and show up in so many different Mexican food creations, that we thought we'd include this dip. We've kept this recipe as low fat as possible.

3/4 cup FAT FREE COTTAGE CHEESE
1/4 cup FAT FREE SOUR CREAM
1/2 ripe AVOCADO, mashed
1 1/2 tsp. LEMON JUICE
1/2 tsp. GARLIC SALT
1/4 tsp. PEPPER
3 Tbsp. SALSA
4 Tbsp. diced GREEN CHILES

In a food processor, blend cottage cheese, sour cream, avocado, lemon juice, garlic salt and pepper until smooth. Add salsa and green chiles and pulse briefly. Transfer to serving bowl. May be served immediately or covered and chilled until ready for use (this will keep in the refrigerator for one or two days.) Serve with baked tortilla chips and your favorite fresh vegetables.

Fat grams per serving = 1

Salsa Blanca

1 pint FAT FREE COTTAGE CHEESE
3 Tbsp. FAT FREE MAYONNAISE
1 cup CHUNKY SALSA

Combine all ingredients. Serve with baked tortilla chips or use as a dip for fresh vegetables.

Fat grams per serving = 0

Nachos

BAKED CORN TORTILLA CHIPS
1 cup shredded LOW FAT CHEDDAR CHEESE
1 can (4 oz.) diced GREEN CHILES
1 med. TOMATO, diced
3 GREEN ONIONS, chopped
2 Tbsp. BLACK OLIVES, chopped

Preheat oven to 350°. On a large oven-proof platter layer tortilla chips, cheese and green chiles. Bake for five minutes or until cheese melts. Remove from oven and sprinkle with tomatoes and onions. Top with black olives. Serve with **SALSA** on the side. Other excellent accompaniments include **FAT FREE SOUR CREAM** and your favorite **DIPS.**

Serves 8.   Fat grams per serving = 2.6

Pico de Gallo

Spanish for "rooster's beak," pico de gallo (PEE-koh day GI-yoh) is a relish made of finely chopped ingredients. This condiment was so named because it was once purportedly eaten with the thumb and finger, an action that resembles a rooster's pecking beak.

3 lg. TOMATOES   **1/2 Tbsp. SALT**
4 JALAPEÑOS   **1 tsp. BLACK PEPPER**
1 lg. ONION   **1/4 cup COLD WATER**
1 lg. GREEN BELL PEPPER   **2 Tbsp. VINEGAR**
2 cloves GARLIC   **1 LIME**
1 bunch fresh CILANTRO

On a cutting board finely chop tomatoes, jalapeños, onion, bell pepper, garlic and cilantro. Place all in glass bowl and mix together. Add salt, pepper, water and vinegar. Squeeze the juice from the lime into the mixture and mix thoroughly. Chill before serving.

Fat grams per serving = 0

Baked Fiesta Dip

1 can (15 oz.) FAT FREE REFRIED BEANS
2 JALAPEÑOS, finely chopped
1 lb. GROUND TURKEY
1 cup shredded LOW FAT JACK CHEESE
1 sm. ONION, chopped
1 GREEN BELL PEPPER, chopped
1 TOMATO, chopped
3 GREEN ONIONS, chopped
BAKED TORTILLA CHIPS

Combine beans and jalapeños and spread on large oven-proof platter (or pizza pan.) Cook ground turkey in a nonstick skillet until brown. Crumble turkey on top of beans, then sprinkle with cheese. Add onion and bell pepper. Bake at 325° for 20 minutes. Top with tomatoes and green onions and serve with tortilla chips.

Serves 16.   Fat grams per serving = 4

Layered Dip

1 can (15 oz.) FAT FREE REFRIED BEANS
1 cup FAT FREE COTTAGE CHEESE
1 cup FAT FREE SOUR CREAM
1/2 cup CHUNKY SALSA
1 can (4 oz.) diced GREEN CHILES, drained
1 TOMATO, chopped
1/2 cup shredded LOW FAT CHEDDAR CHEESE
BAKED TORTILLA CHIPS

Spread beans evenly in a 9-inch pie plate. Spread cottage cheese over beans. Combine sour cream and salsa and layer over cottage cheese. Cover and chill for at least two hours. Just before serving sprinkle with chiles and tomato and top with cheddar cheese. Serve with tortilla chips.

Serves 12.   Fat grams per serving = <1

Breakfasts

Huevos con Chiles Verde (Eggs with Green Chiles) 22

Skillet Potatoes 22

Huevos Rancheros 23

Low Fat Chorizo 23

Baked Chile Relleno 24

Torta de Chile Verde (Green Chile Omelet) 25

Corn Pudding 25

Breakfast Burritos 26

Mission Burritos 26

Huevos con Chiles Verde
(Eggs with Green Chiles)

This scrambled egg dish is a great eye-opener when served with salsa and warm corn tortillas. For a spicier morning dish, substitute jalapeños for the green chiles.

1 Tbsp. LOW FAT MARGARINE
1 can (4 oz.) diced GREEN CHILES, drained or
    2 oz. diced JALAPEÑOS
3 Tbsp. chopped ONIONS
1 carton (8 oz.) EGG SUBSTITUTE
1/2 tsp. GARLIC SALT
PEPPER to taste
1 sm. TOMATO, finely chopped

In a skillet sauté chiles and onions in margarine. Add garlic salt and pepper to egg substitute. Stir into chiles and onions and cook until eggs reach desired consistency. Sprinkle tomatoes over top and serve warm.

Serves 4.   Fat grams per serving = 1.5

Skillet Potatoes

2 Tbsp. LOW FAT MARGARINE
1 med. ONION, chopped
1 GREEN BELL PEPPER, chopped
4 POTATOES, peeled and diced
1/2 tsp. GARLIC SALT
1/4 tsp. PEPPER
1/4 tsp. ground OREGANO
1/4 tsp. CHILI POWDER

In a large frying pan or skillet sauté onions and bell pepper in margarine. When onions and pepper are tender, add diced potatoes and seasonings. Cover and cook over medium heat, stirring occasionally. When potatoes have softened, uncover and fry to desired crispness. Serve with plenty of salsa.

Serves 8.   Fat grams per serving = 1.5

Huevos Rancheros

4 (7-inch) FLOUR TORTILLAS
1 1/2 cups cooked, mashed PINTO BEANS
4 EGGS
3/4 cup shredded LOW FAT CHEDDAR CHEESE
CHUNKY SALSA

Arrange tortillas on cookie sheet. Spread beans on tortillas. Fry eggs as desired (over-easy, scrambled, sunny-side up) in non-stick skillet. Leave eggs slightly undercooked as they will be getting additional heat when broiled. Arrange eggs over beans. Sprinkle cheese evenly over eggs. Place under broiler just long enough to melt cheese. Remove to serving platters and add salsa to taste.

Serves 4.   Fat grams per serving = 9

Note: **Green Chile Sauce** (see page 54), or **Red Chile Sauce** (see page 55) can be ladled over eggs before placing under the broiler.

Low Fat Chorizo

Great scrambled with eggs or potatoes!

1 lb. ground CHICKEN or TURKEY
1 tsp. crushed RED PEPPER
1 tsp. ground CHILTEPIN
2 Tbsp. CHILI POWDER
1/4 tsp. CUMIN
1/2 tsp. GARLIC POWDER
1 tsp. SALT
1/2 tsp. PEPPER
3 Tbsp. VINEGAR

Combine all ingredients in a glass bowl. Mix thoroughly. Cover and refrigerate for several hours. When ready to use, fry in a hot skillet with a small amount of oil.

Serves 6.   Fat grams per serving = 3.9

Baked Chile Relleno

We have this recipe in our breakfast section, however, it makes a great main dish as well and it's perfect for bringing to a potluck.

1/2 cup NON-FAT DRY MILK
2 cups SKIM MILK
3 Tbsp. FLOUR
2 cartons (8 oz. each) EGG SUBSTITUTE
1/4 cup SALSA
6 CORN TORTILLAS
1 can (7 oz.) diced GREEN CHILES
3/4 cup shredded LOW FAT CHEDDAR CHEESE
3/4 cup shredded LOW FAT JACK CHEESE
1/2 cup finely chopped GREEN ONION

Preheat oven to 325°. Combine dry milk and skim milk and stir in flour. Blend thoroughly. Add egg substitute and salsa. Lightly spray a 9 x 13 baking dish with vegetable spray. Layer with corn tortillas, green chiles, cheeses and onion. Pour egg mixture on top. Bake for 1 hour. Remove from oven and let set for 10 minutes before serving.

Serves 10.   Fat grams per serving = 2.7

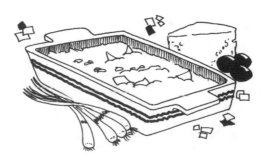

Torta de Chile Verde

(Green Chile Omelet)

6 EGGS
6 Tbsp. WATER
1/2 tsp. SALT
1/4 tsp. PAPRIKA
1/4 tsp. PEPPER
2 ANAHEIM or NEW MEXICO CHILES, seeded and sliced
1/2 cup shredded LOW FAT CHEDDAR CHEESE

In a bowl, separate eggs. Place egg whites in smaller bowl and beat egg yolks thoroughly. Add water and seasonings to the egg yolks and mix well. Whip egg whites until stiff. Fold egg whites into yolks. Pour egg mixture into a nonstick skillet and cook over medium heat until edges begin to brown (surface of eggs should just begin to set). Add chiles and cheese and fold omelet in half. Continue to cook until cheese melts. Do not overcook. Remove to serving platter and cut into wedges. Serve with salsa and warm tortillas.

Serves 6.   Fat grams per serving = 5.5

Corn Pudding

4 cups SKIM MILK
1/2 cup CORNMEAL
1/2 cup MAPLE SYRUP

2 EGGS
1/2 tsp. CINNAMON
1/3 cup BROWN SUGAR

In a saucepan, heat milk over medium heat until very hot, but not boiling. Stir cornmeal into milk and simmer gently for 20 minutes, stirring occasionally. In a medium bowl, combine remaining ingredients. Add to cornmeal mixture and blend thoroughly. Pour into a lightly oiled oven-proof baking dish. Bake in a 325° oven for 1 hour. Let stand to set before serving. Serve warm or chilled.

Serves 6.   Fat grams per serving = 1.3

Breakfast Burritos

A quick and easy way to start the day! These tasty burritos can be rolled and eaten out of hand.

2 tsp. LOW FAT MARGARINE
1/2 sm. ONION, chopped
1 can (4 oz.) diced GREEN
   CHILES, drained
1/2 cup cooked LEAN HAM, cubed

1 carton EGG SUBSTITUTE
SALT and PEPPER to taste
SALSA, to taste
4 (10-inch) FLOUR
   TORTILLAS

     In a skillet, heat margarine and sauté onions until tender. Add chiles and ham and continue to fry. Add egg substitute, salt and pepper to skillet mixture. Scramble over medium heat. As eggs solidify add salsa. Warm tortillas. Place equal amounts of egg mixture onto each tortilla and roll burrito style.

     Serves 4.   Fat grams per serving = 5.5

Mission Burritos

2 tsp. LOW FAT MARGARINE
1/2 sm. ONION, chopped
1 can (4 oz.) diced GREEN CHILES, drained
1 carton (8 oz.) EGG SUBSTITUTE
1/2 tsp. GARLIC SALT
1/3 cup shredded LOW FAT CHEDDAR CHEESE
4 (10-inch) FLOUR TORTILLAS
ALFALFA SPROUTS
1 med. TOMATO, chopped
SALSA

     In a skillet, sauté onions in margarine until tender. Add chiles. Add egg substitute and garlic salt to onions and chiles. Scramble over medium heat, sprinkle with cheese and cook until eggs are desired consistency. Warm tortillas. Place equal amounts of egg mixture onto each tortilla. Add sprouts, tomato and salsa. Roll up burrito style.

     Serves 4.   Fat grams per serving = 5.5

Soups & Salads

Gazpacho 28
Tortilla Soup 28
Pinto Bean Soup 29
Hearty Bean Soup 30
Black Bean & Rice Soup 30
Caldo de Pollo (Chicken Soup) 31
Menudo 32
Sopa de Papas (Potato Soup)...................................33
Albondigas (Meatball Soup).....................................34
Taco Soup 35
Sopa de Fideo (Pasta Soup) 35
Ensalada de Pepiño (Cucumber Salad) 36
Jicama Salad 36
Chicken Taco Salad 37
Ensalada de Tres Frijoles (Three Bean Salad) 37
Fiesta Salad 38
Potato Salad 38
Corn Salad 39
Black Bean Salad 39
Turkey & Rice Salad 40

Gazpacho

4 TOMATOES, chopped
1 lg. CUCUMBER, peeled
   and chopped
1 GREEN BELL PEPPER, seeded
   and chopped
1 bunch GREEN ONIONS,
   finely chopped

3 cups TOMATO JUICE
1 clove GARLIC, minced
1/2 tsp. OREGANO
1/2 tsp. TABASCO®
1 Tbsp. LEMON JUICE
SALT and PEPPER to taste
Fresh CILANTRO

Mix all ingredients, except cilantro, in a large glass bowl. Cover and chill for at least four hours. Pour into individual bowls and garnish with fresh cilantro.

Serves 4.

Fat grams per serving = 0

Tortilla Soup

6 CORN TORTILLAS
1 can (15 oz.) FAT FREE CHICKEN BROTH
2 cups WATER
1 ONION, chopped
1 clove GARLIC, minced
3 CARROTS, cut into 1-inch strips
2 stalks CELERY, sliced
1 can (4 oz.) diced GREEN CHILES
1/8 tsp. CUMIN
1/2 tsp. OREGANO
1/4 cup chopped CILANTRO
SALT and PEPPER to taste
1/3 cup shredded LOW FAT JACK CHEESE

Cut tortillas into thin strips and bake, on a cookie sheet, in a 400° oven until crisp. Combine chicken broth, water, vegetables and seasonings and simmer for 30 minutes. When ready to serve place equal amounts of tortilla strips in bottom of each bowl and ladle soup into bowls. Garnish with cheese.

Serves 6.

Fat grams per serving = 1

Pinto Bean Soup

1 lb. dried PINTO BEANS
WATER
1 lg. ONION, chopped
1 clove GARLIC, minced
1 JALAPEÑO, seeded and chopped
1/2 tsp. OREGANO
1/4 tsp. CUMIN
dash of CAYENNE
1/2 tsp. BLACK PEPPER
SALT to taste

Sort through beans and wash thoroughly. Cover with water and allow to soak overnight. Drain and rinse. Cover beans with fresh water. Add remaining ingredients and bring to boil. Reduce heat to low and cover with tight-fitting lid. Continue to cook until beans are tender (approximately 2-3 hours.) Stir at least every 30 minutes and add water as necessary (beans should always be covered with liquid.) Place in serving bowls and garnish with **chopped TOMATOES** and **sprigs of CILANTRO.**

Serves 6.   Fat grams per serving = 0

Hearty Bean Soup

1 can (15 oz.) PINTO BEANS
1 can (16 oz.) TOMATOES
1 can (4 oz.) diced GREEN CHILES
1 ONION, chopped
2 CARROTS, sliced
2 stalks CELERY, sliced
2 cups WATER
2 cups cooked LEAN HAM, cubed
1 tsp. GARLIC SALT
1 tsp. CHILI POWDER

Combine all ingredients in a large pot and bring to a boil. Reduce heat, cover and simmer for 30 minutes.

Serves 6.   Fat grams per serving = 4

Black Bean & Rice Soup

1 ONION, chopped
2 stalks CELERY, diced
1 RED BELL PEPPER, diced
3 CARROTS, diced
2 cans (15 oz. each) FAT FREE CHICKEN BROTH
2 cans (15 oz. each) FAT FREE BLACK BEANS, drained
1 cup INSTANT RICE
1 cup SALSA
1/2 tsp. GARLIC SALT
1/2 tsp. OREGANO
1/8 tsp. CAYENNE
1/4 tsp. BLACK PEPPER

In a large saucepan cook onion, celery, bell pepper and carrots in chicken broth until tender. Stir in beans, rice, salsa and seasonings. Bring to a boil, turn off heat, cover and let stand 5 minutes.

Serves 6.   Fat grams per serving = 0

Caldo de Pollo

(Chicken Soup)

Chicken soup is not only good for your soul,
but good for your body, too!

4 CHICKEN BREASTS, with skin removed
8 cups WATER
2 ANAHEIM or NEW MEXICO CHILES
1 ONION, quartered
4 stalks CELERY, diced in large pieces
4 CARROTS, sliced in large pieces
1 BAY LEAF
1/2 tsp. GARLIC SALT
1/2 tsp. CAYENNE
1/2 cup fresh, chopped CILANTRO
1/2 tsp. CUMIN
2 ZUCCHINIS, sliced in large pieces
SALT and PEPPER to taste

In a large pot cover chicken breasts with water and bring to boil. Cook for 10 minutes, skimming off any fat that floats to the surface. Add seeded and diced chiles (be sure to wear rubber gloves and do not touch your face!) Add onion, celery, carrots, bay leaf and seasonings. Reduce heat, cover pot and simmer for 30 minutes. Remove chicken, debone and add back to pot. Add zucchini and salt and pepper and continue simmering until vegetables are tender. Remove bay leaf before serving.

Serves 8.   Fat grams per serving = 1.5

Menudo

Menudo is rumored to be a great cure for hangovers.

2 lbs. BEEF TRIPE
2 qts. CHICKEN BROTH, defatted
2 lg. ONIONS, chopped
6 cloves GARLIC, minced
2 cans (15 oz. each) HOMINY, drained
SALT and PEPPER to taste
1 bunch GREEN ONIONS, chopped
1 bunch fresh CILANTRO, chopped

Clean, scrape and trim all visible fat from tripe. Place in a large pot, cover with salted water and boil for 2 hours. Drain and rinse. Cut into small squares. Place back in pot and add chicken broth, onions and garlic. Bring to a boil, reduce heat, cover and simmer for approximately 1 hour or until meat is tender. Add hominy, salt and pepper and simmer for 30 minutes. Just before serving add green onions and cilantro. Serve with warm tortillas.

Serves 6.   Fat grams per serving = 5.3

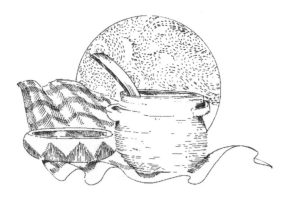

Sopa de Papas

(Potato Soup)

6 lg. POTATOES
1 ONION, chopped
1 GREEN BELL PEPPER, chopped
1 can (4 oz.) diced GREEN CHILES
2 stalks CELERY, sliced
2 cloves GARLIC, minced
6 cups WATER
1 can (15 oz.) FAT FREE CHICKEN BROTH
SALT and PEPPER to taste
1/4 tsp. CAYENNE
2 Tbsp. CORNSTARCH
1/4 cup WATER
1/2 lb. shredded LOW FAT CHEDDAR CHEESE
1 bunch fresh CILANTRO, chopped

Wash and cube potatoes (peel if desired). Place potatoes, onion, bell pepper, green chiles, celery, garlic, 6 cups water, chicken broth, salt, pepper and cayenne into a large pot. Bring to a boil, lower heat, cover and simmer until potatoes are tender. Stir occasionally. To thicken, add cornstarch to 1/4 cup water and blend till smooth. Stir into simmering soup. When serving, sprinkle with shredded cheese and fresh cilantro.

Serves 8.   Fat grams per serving = 4.5

Note: Lean cooked ham or shredded chicken or turkey breast can be added for a heartier soup.

Albondigas
(Meatball Soup)

Soup
   2 qts. CHICKEN BROTH, defatted
   1 ONION, diced
   3 stalks CELERY, sliced
   3 CARROTS, sliced
   1 cup chopped fresh CILANTRO
   1/2 cup mild SALSA

Combine all ingredients in a soup pot and simmer for 10 minutes.

Meatballs
   1 lb. GROUND TURKEY
   3 Tbsp. uncooked INSTANT RICE
   1/2 cup finely minced ONION
   1/4 cup chopped fresh CILANTRO
   1/2 tsp. GARLIC SALT
   1/2 tsp. OREGANO

Mix all ingredients together and form into small balls. Bring soup to a boil and carefully place meatballs into soup. Cover and reduce heat and simmer for 30 minutes.

Serves 6.   Fat grams per serving = 9

Taco Soup

1 lb. GROUND TURKEY
1 ONION, chopped
2 cups WATER
1 can (16 oz.) STEWED TOMATOES
1 can (16 oz.) KIDNEY BEANS
1 can (8 oz.) TOMATO SAUCE
1 pkg. TACO SEASONING MIX
1/2 cup shredded LOW FAT JACK CHEESE
FAT FREE SOUR CREAM

Sauté turkey and onion in a large saucepan until onion is tender. Add water, tomatoes, beans, tomato sauce, and taco seasoning. Bring to a boil, reduce heat, cover and simmer for 30 minutes. Ladle into serving bowls and garnish with a sprinkle of cheese and a dollop of sour cream.

Serves 8.   Fat grams per serving = 6.7

Sopa de Fideo
(Pasta Soup)

1 pkg. (8 oz.) FIDEO PASTA
1 sm. ONION, finely chopped
2 CARROTS, finely diced
2 stalks CELERY, finely diced
1 can (16 oz.) STEWED TOMATOES, chopped
1/2 cup frozen PEAS
4 cups WATER
2 CHICKEN BOUILLON CUBES
1/4 tsp. GARLIC POWDER

Combine all ingredients in a soup pot. Bring to a boil, stirring occasionally. Continue to cook until pasta is at desired tenderness.

Serves 4.   Fat grams per serving = 0

Ensalada de Pepiño

(Cucumber Salad)

4 CUCUMBERS, peeled and sliced
1 sm. RED ONION, sliced into thin rings
1 cup JICAMA, sliced
1 TOMATO, sliced
2 Tbsp. SUGAR
2 Tbsp. LEMON JUICE
2 Tbsp. VINEGAR
PAPRIKA

Combine all ingredients, except paprika, and chill. Refrigerate overnight for best flavor. Before serving toss gently and sprinkle with paprika.

Serves 6.   Fat grams per serving = 0

Jicama Salad

1 1/2 cups JICAMA strips
1 sm. RED ONION, chopped
1 GREEN BELL PEPPER, seeded and chopped
1 Tbsp. VINEGAR
JUICE of one LEMON
1/4 tsp. CAYENNE
SALT and PEPPER to taste

Combine all ingredients. Refrigerate for at least two hours, preferably overnight. Toss gently before serving.

Serves 4.   Fat grams per serving = 0

Chicken Taco Salad

2 boneless, skinless CHICKEN BREASTS
1/2 tsp. GARLIC SALT
1 Tbsp. CHILI POWDER
LETTUCE, torn into bite-size pieces
1 CUCUMBER, peeled and diced
1 cup shredded LOW FAT CHEDDAR CHEESE
1 cup CHUNKY SALSA
1 TOMATO, chopped
3 GREEN ONIONS, chopped
FAT FREE RANCH DRESSING
BAKED TORTILLA CHIPS

Sprinkle chicken with garlic salt and chili powder. Broil for 2 minutes or until done. Cool and cut into strips. In a bowl, toss lettuce with chicken, cucumber and cheese. To serve, top with salsa, tomato, green onions, dressing and crushed tortilla chips.

Serves 6.   Fat grams per serving = 4

Ensalada de Tres Frijoles
(Three Bean Salad)

1 can (15 oz.) KIDNEY BEANS, drained and rinsed
1 can (15 oz.) FAT FREE BLACK BEANS, drained and rinsed
1 can (15 oz.) GARBANZO BEANS, drained and rinsed
1 RED ONION, thinly sliced
2 stalks CELERY, sliced
1 TOMATO, chopped
1 cup THICK & CHUNKY SALSA
shredded LETTUCE

In a large bowl combine all ingredients, except for lettuce. Cover and chill for at least 1 hour. Serve over shredded lettuce.

Serves 8.   Fat grams per serving = <1

Fiesta Salad

8 roasted, peeled and seeded GREEN CHILES, chopped
2 TOMATOES, sliced
1 sm. RED ONION, coarsely chopped
1 CUCUMBER, peeled and sliced
1 each GREEN, RED & YELLOW BELL PEPPER, chopped
1/4 cup chopped, fresh CILANTRO
3 Tbsp. SALSA
2 Tbsp. LEMON JUICE
1/2 tsp. GARLIC SALT
1/4 tsp. PEPPER
1/4 tsp. CUMIN

Combine all ingredients and chill for at least one hour. Serve with baked tortilla chips or on a bed of lettuce.

Serves 6.   Fat grams per serving = 0

Potato Salad

8 NEW POTATOES, cooked
  and cubed
3 stalks CELERY, diced
2 CARROTS, shredded
3 GREEN ONIONS, sliced
1/2 RED BELL PEPPER, chopped
2 JALAPEÑOS, thinly sliced
1/2 cup FAT FREE MAYONNAISE

1/2 cup FAT FREE SOUR
  CREAM
1/4 tsp. GARLIC POWDER
1/4 tsp. CUMIN
SALT and PEPPER to taste
1 Tbsp. LEMON JUICE
PAPRIKA
CILANTRO

In a large bowl combine potatoes, celery, carrots, onions, bell pepper and jalapeños. In a small bowl blend mayonnaise, sour cream, garlic powder, cumin, salt, pepper and lemon juice. Pour over vegetables and mix thoroughly. Sprinkle with paprika and garnish with cilantro. Chill until ready to serve.

Serves 6.   Fat grams per serving = 0

Corn Salad

2 cans (15 oz. each) CORN, drained
1 can (4 oz.) diced GREEN CHILES, drained
1 sm. RED ONION, sliced into thin rings
4 GREEN ONIONS, chopped
1/2 cup chopped GREEN BELL PEPPER
2 TOMATOES, chopped
1/2 tsp. GARLIC SALT
1/4 tsp. CUMIN
1/4 cup VINEGAR
Juice of half of a LEMON
1 Tbsp. SUGAR
LETTUCE LEAVES

Combine all ingredients, except lettuce leaves, in a bowl. Mix thoroughly. Cover and chill well until ready to serve. Toss lightly to redistribute the dressing. Serve on a bed of lettuce.

Serves 6.   Fat grams per serving = <1

Black Bean Salad

1 can (15 oz.) FAT FREE BLACK BEANS, drained and rinsed
1 can (4 oz.) diced GREEN CHILES, drained
4 GREEN ONIONS, cut into 1/2-inch pieces
2 TOMATOES, chopped
1/4 tsp. GARLIC SALT
PEPPER, to taste
1 Tbsp. LEMON JUICE
2 Tbsp. SALSA
1/2 head LETTUCE, shredded

Combine all ingredients in a large bowl and toss well. Refrigerate for at least an hour or until thoroughly chilled.

Serves 4.   Fat grams per serving = 0

Turkey & Rice Salad

1 lb. GROUND TURKEY
1 sm. ONION, finely chopped
1/2 tsp. CHILI POWDER
1/2 tsp. GARLIC SALT
1/2 tsp. CUMIN
1/2 tsp. OREGANO
4 cups cooked RICE
1 head ICEBERG LETTUCE, shredded
3/4 cup shredded LOW FAT JACK CHEESE
2 TOMATOES, chopped
3 GREEN ONIONS, chopped
SALSA
FAT FREE SOUR CREAM
BAKED TORTILLA CHIPS

In a large skillet, over medium heat, brown turkey with onion, chili powder, garlic salt, cumin and oregano. Add cooked rice and stir, making sure meat has crumbled. Remove from heat and allow to cool. In a large bowl, combine lettuce, cheese, tomatoes and green onions. Add turkey-rice mixture and toss lightly. When ready to serve, garnish with salsa, sour cream and tortilla chips.

Serves 8.   Fat grams per serving = 7.1

Reminder: For all recipes that call for canned beans, a variety of *fat free* and *low fat* beans are now available at your supermarket. These are the beans that are reflected in our nutritional analyses.

Side Dishes

Frijoles (Beans) 42

Spanish Rice 42

Calabacitas (Squash) 43

Calabacitas con Jamón (Squash with Ham) 43

Green Chile Mashed Potatoes 44

Sweet Potatoes 44

Border Pasta 45

Chile Rice 45

Chile Cornbread 46

Hominy con Chile 46

Papas Verde (Green Potatoes) 47

Papas Colorado (Red Potatoes) 47

Black Beans & Corn 48

Frijoles del Mar 48

Stuffed Baked Potatoes 49

Mexican Casserole 49

Mexi-Macaroni 50

Arroz de Mexico (Mexican Rice) 51

Chili Colorado 51

Fiesta Hominy 52

Lemon Rice 52

Frijoles
(Beans)

1 lb. dried PINTO BEANS, sorted and rinsed	2 cloves GARLIC, minced
WATER	1/4 tsp. OREGANO
	PEPPER to taste
1 lg. ONION, chopped	SALT to taste

Place beans in a large pot and add water to cover. Soak beans overnight. (For quicker use, bring to boil for five minutes, remove from heat and let soak, covered for one hour.) Drain beans. Cover with fresh water and add onion, garlic, oregano and pepper. Bring to a boil, reduce heat and simmer, covered, until beans are tender (approximately 3 hours.) Add water as necessary. To avoid making the beans too tough, season with salt shortly before beans have reached desired tenderness.

Serves 6.   Fat grams per serving = 0

Spanish Rice

1 1/2 cups uncooked WHITE RICE
2 1/2 Tbsp. LOW FAT MARGARINE
1 ONION, chopped
1 sm. GREEN BELL PEPPER, diced
2 cloves GARLIC, minced
1 can (8 oz.) TOMATO SAUCE
3 cups WATER
1/2 tsp. OREGANO
1/4 tsp. CHILI POWDER
SALT to taste

In a large nonstick skillet, brown rice in margarine. Add onion, bell pepper and garlic. Sauté for two minutes. Add tomato sauce, water and seasonings. Bring to a boil, turn down heat to simmer and cover and cook until rice is tender and all moisture is absorbed.

Serves 6.   Fat grams per serving = 0

Calabacitas
(Squash)

This is a great accompaniment for meat dishes.

6 ZUCCHINIS, sliced
1 ONION, chopped
2 cloves GARLIC, minced
1 lg. TOMATO, chopped
1 can (15 oz.) WHOLE KERNEL CORN, drained
1 can (16 oz.) STEWED TOMATOES, chopped
SALT to taste
1/2 cup shredded LOW FAT JACK CHEESE

Preheat oven to 350°. Place all ingredients, except cheese, into casserole dish. Cover and bake until vegetables are tender, approximately 20 minutes (or, microwave on HIGH for approximately 10 minutes.) Remove from heat and sprinkle with cheese. Toss lightly and serve hot.

Serves 8.   Fat grams per serving = 1.4

Calabacitas con Jamón
(Squash with Ham)

2 lbs. SUMMER SQUASH, diced
1 Tbsp. LOW FAT MARGARINE
1/2 ONION, diced
2 TOMATOES, diced
1 can (4 oz.) diced GREEN CHILES
2 cups cooked LEAN HAM, cubed
1/4 tsp. GARLIC POWDER
SALT and PEPPER to taste

Cook squash until tender and drain. In a large nonstick skillet sauté onion in margarine until tender. Add squash, tomatoes, chiles, ham and seasonings. Mix well, cover and simmer for five minutes.

Serves 6.   Fat grams per serving = 5

Green Chile Mashed Potatoes

4 RUSSET POTATOES
1 tsp. OLIVE OIL
2 cloves GARLIC, minced
1 RED ONION, chopped
1 can (4 oz.) diced GREEN CHILES
1/2 cup FAT FREE SOUR CREAM
1/4 cup fresh CILANTRO, chopped
SALT and PEPPER to taste

Wash and cut potatoes into 2-inch pieces. Place in pot and cover with cold water. Boil for 20 minutes or until tender. While potatoes are cooking, sauté garlic and onion in olive oil in a nonstick skillet. When onion is tender add green chiles. Drain and mash potatoes. Stir in sour cream and add onion, chiles and cilantro. Season with salt and pepper and mix well.

Serves 4.

Fat grams per serving = 0

Sweet Potatoes

4 medium SWEET POTATOES
1 cup BROWN SUGAR
1 can (17 oz.) PINEAPPLE chunks, drained
2 cups WATER
2 Tbsp. grated ORANGE PEEL
1 tsp. CINNAMON
1/2 tsp. NUTMEG

Wash and peel potatoes and cut into 1 1/2-inch chunks. In a large saucepan mix brown sugar, pineapple, water, orange peel, cinnamon and nutmeg. Bring to a boil. Add sweet potatoes, cover and reduce heat and simmer for 30 minutes or until tender. Serve warm or chilled.

Serves 6-8.

Fat grams per serving = <1

Border Pasta

8 oz. PASTA
1 pkg. (8 oz.) FAT FREE CREAM CHEESE
3 Tbsp. diced GREEN CHILES
1/2 cup chopped fresh CILANTRO
1/2 tsp. GARLIC SALT

Cook pasta according to package directions. In a saucepan combine cream cheese, green chiles, cilantro and garlic salt. Gently warm over low heat, stirring to blend ingredients. Pour pasta over cream cheese sauce and stir to mix thoroughly. Serve warm.

Serves 4.   Fat grams per serving = 1

Chile Rice

Try this recipe as an alternative to Spanish rice.

3 cups cooked RICE
1 can (7 oz.) diced GREEN CHILES
2 cups FAT FREE SOUR CREAM
1 cup shredded LOW FAT CHEDDAR CHEESE

Combine all ingredients and pour into a lightly oiled baking dish. Bake in oven at 350° for 30 minutes.

Serves 4.   Fat grams per serving = 4.9

Chile Cornbread

1 cup CORNMEAL
1 cup FLOUR
1 Tbsp. BAKING POWDER
1 tsp. SALT
1 1/2 cups SKIM MILK
2 EGGS, slightly beaten
1 can (4 oz.) diced GREEN CHILES, drained
1 can (15 oz.) CORN, drained
4 Tbsp. SALSA
1 cup shredded FAT FREE CHEDDAR CHEESE

Mix all ingredients together in a large bowl. Pour into a nonstick 9 x 13 baking pan. Bake at 350° for 45 minutes, or until toothpick inserted in center comes out clean. Serve warm or allow to cool.

Serves 12.   Fat grams per serving = 1.2

Hominy con Chile

Use this recipe in place of potatoes or rice.

2 cans (15 oz. each) HOMINY
1 can (7 oz.) diced GREEN CHILES
1 can (10.5 oz.) LOW FAT CREAM OF MUSHROOM SOUP
1 cup FAT FREE SOUR CREAM
1/8 tsp. CUMIN
1/4 tsp. PEPPER
1 Tbsp. dried CILANTRO
1 cup shredded LOW FAT CHEDDAR CHEESE

Preheat oven to 350°. Pour hominy into a colander, rinse well with water and allow to drain. In a large bowl combine hominy, chiles, soup, sour cream, seasonings and 1/2 cup cheese. Mix well and pour into a nonstick baking dish. Sprinkle remaining cheese on top and bake for 45 minutes.

Serves 8.   Fat grams per serving = 3.5

Papas Verde
(Green Potatoes)

1 ONION, chopped
2 JALAPEÑOS, seeded and diced
1 clove GARLIC, minced
1 Tbsp. VEGETABLE OIL
2 lbs. POTATOES, cut into 1-inch cubes
2 cans (8 oz. each) TOMATO SAUCE
1 can (7 oz.) diced GREEN CHILES
2 Tbsp. CORNSTARCH
1/4 cup WATER

In a large skillet, sauté onion, jalapeños and garlic in vegetable oil. Add potatoes and continue to cook. When potatoes begin to brown, add tomato sauce and green chiles. Cover and simmer for 30 minutes. In a small bowl dissolve cornstarch in 1/4 cup water and stir into potato mixture to thicken sauce. Serve with warm tortillas.

Serves 6.   Fat grams per serving = 2.3

Papas Colorado
(Red Potatoes)

2 lbs. POTATOES, cut into 1-inch cubes
3 Tbsp. chopped fresh CILANTRO
1 tsp. GARLIC SALT
4 Tbsp. SALSA
2 Tbsp. crushed RED PEPPER FLAKES

Boil potatoes and drain thoroughly. Return potatoes to cooking pot and add remaining ingredients. Gently stir to coat potatoes. Serve hot.

Serves 6.   Fat grams per serving = 0

Black Beans & Corn

This delicious side dish is great served warm and also tastes wonderful as a chilled salad accompaniment!

2 cans (15 oz. each) FAT FREE BLACK BEANS, drained
2 cans (15 oz. each) CORN, drained
1 can (15 oz.) MEXICAN STYLE STEWED TOMATOES
1 RED ONION, chopped
1 bunch GREEN ONIONS, chopped
1/2 bunch CILANTRO, chopped
1/2 tsp. CHILI POWDER
1/2 tsp. GARLIC SALT
1/4 tsp. CUMIN
1/4 tsp. PEPPER

Combine all ingredients in a large saucepan and heat on medium heat until warmed through.

Serves 8.   Fat grams per serving = <1

Frijoles del Mar

We adapted this recipe from a quaint little restaurant in Cabo San Lucas.

1 can (15 oz.) PINTO BEANS, drained and rinsed
2 cans (6 oz. each) water-packed TUNA, drained
6 GREEN ONIONS, chopped
2 cloves GARLIC, minced
3 stalks CELERY, chopped
1/4 cup chopped fresh CILANTRO
2 Tbsp. CHILI POWDER
1/2 tsp. CUMIN
1/2 cup FAT FREE MAYONNAISE

In a large bowl combine all ingredients and toss to blend thoroughly. This dish can be served heated or chilled.

Serves 6.   Fat grams per serving = <1

Stuffed Baked Potatoes

3 lg. RUSSET POTATOES
1/2 cup FAT FREE COTTAGE CHEESE
1/2 cup FAT FREE SOUR CREAM
1 can (4 oz.) diced GREEN CHILES
1/2 tsp. GARLIC SALT
1/2 bunch fresh CILANTRO, chopped
PAPRIKA

Bake potatoes and allow to cool until easy to handle. Slice in half lengthwise and scoop out centers, leaving 1/2-inch rim, and set shells aside. Mash potato centers and combine with cottage cheese and sour cream, blending thoroughly. Stir in green chiles, garlic salt and cilantro. Fill potato skins with mixture, sprinkle with paprika and place in 350° oven for 10-15 minutes, or until crispy on top.

Serves 6.   Fat grams per serving = 0

Mexican Casserole

1 lb. GROUND TURKEY, cooked
4 cups cooked PINTO BEANS
1 can (15 oz.) STEWED TOMATOES
1/2 GREEN BELL PEPPER, chopped

1/2 ONION, chopped
1/2 tsp. GARLIC SALT
1 tsp. CHILI POWDER
1/4 tsp. CUMIN

Combine all ingredients and turn into a baking dish. Bake in a 350° oven for 1 hour.

Serves 8.   Fat grams per serving = 5.6

Mexi-Macaroni

This is a great way to spice up your macaroni and cheese!

1 Tbsp. VEGETABLE OIL
1/2 ONION, chopped
3 Tbsp. diced GREEN CHILES
1 Tbsp. FLOUR
1 tsp. GARLIC SALT
1 tsp. CHILI POWDER
1/4 tsp. CUMIN
1 pkg. (8 oz.) ELBOW MACARONI
3 1/2 cups SKIM MILK
1/2 cup FAT FREE COTTAGE CHEESE
1 cup shredded LOW FAT CHEDDAR CHEESE

In a large skillet sauté onion in oil. Add green chiles and stir in flour, garlic salt, chili powder and cumin. Add macaroni and milk. Cover and bring to a boil. Reduce heat and simmer 15 minutes or until macaroni is tender, stirring occasionally. Add cottage cheese and cheddar cheese and heat until cheese melts.

Serves 6.   Fat grams per serving = 6

Arroz de Mexico

(Mexican Rice)

2 Tbsp. VEGETABLE OIL
2 cups uncooked RICE
3 cups FAT FREE CHICKEN BROTH
1/2 ONION, chopped
1/2 GREEN BELL PEPPER, chopped
1 cup frozen PEAS
1 can (15 oz.) MEXICAN STYLE STEWED TOMATOES
1 CARROT, grated
1/2 tsp. GARLIC SALT
1/4 tsp. CUMIN

Heat oil in a large skillet and sauté rice until golden. Add 1/2 cup broth, onion and bell pepper and sauté for 2 more minutes. Stir in remaining broth, peas, tomatoes, carrot and seasonings. Bring to a boil, reduce heat, cover and simmer for 20 minutes or until broth is absorbed.

Serves 8.   Fat grams per serving = 8.4

Chili Colorado

A great accompaniment to tacos and burritos. This is also a great filling for tortillas.

1 lb. lean PORK TENDERLOIN, cubed
1 Tbsp. OIL
2 Tbsp. FLOUR
1 RED BELL PEPPER, seeded
    and cut into large chunks
1 ONION, quartered

2 POTATOES, cut into
    large chunks
3 cups WATER
3 Tbsp. CHILI POWDER
1/2 tsp. GARLIC SALT
1/4 tsp. CUMIN

In a large pot, brown meat in oil. Sprinkle and stir in flour. Add pepper, onion and potatoes. Add water and bring to a boil. Reduce heat, stir in seasonings, cover and simmer 2 hours or until meat is tender.

Serves 6.   Fat grams per serving = 5.2

Fiesta Hominy

*Try serving this wonderful side dish as an alternative
to rice or potatoes.*

2 Tbsp. FLOUR
2 Tbsp. OIL
2 Tbsp. diced ONION
3 Tbsp. diced GREEN BELL PEPPER
1 TOMATO, sliced

1 can (29 oz.) HOMINY
2 cups WATER
1/2 tsp. GARLIC SALT
1/4 tsp. OREGANO
dash PEPPER

Brown flour in oil. Add onion and sauté. Add bell pepper
and tomato and stir over medium heat. Stir in drained hominy,
water and seasonings. Cover and simmer for 15 minutes over
medium heat, stirring occasionally.

Serves 6.

Fat grams per serving = 5

Lemon Rice

*The delicate citrus flavor of this rice dish provides a nice
balance to seafood entrées.*

2 cups WATER
1/4 cup LEMON JUICE
1/4 cup LIME JUICE
2 Tbsp. grated LEMON RIND
1/2 tsp. GARLIC SALT
1/4 tsp. OREGANO
1 cup regular uncooked RICE
fresh CILANTRO, to taste

In a saucepan, combine water, lemon and lime juices, lemon
rind, garlic salt and oregano and bring to a boil. Reduce heat
and stir in rice. Cover and simmer for 30 minutes or until all
liquid has been absorbed. Just before serving, while still hot,
add fresh, chopped cilantro and toss gently.

Serves 4.

Fat grams per serving = <1

Main Dishes

Green Chile Sauce 54
Red Chile Sauce 55
Muy Pronto Salsa Roja (Quick Red Sauce) 55
Beefy Tostadas 56
Bean Tostadas 56
Chicken Tostadas 57
Mexican Pizza 57
Chicken Enchiladas 58
Beef Enchiladas 58
Cheese Enchiladas 59
Chicken Enchilada Casserole 59
Sonoran Enchiladas 60
Taco Shells 61
Chicken Tacos 61
Beef Tacos 61
Turkey Tacos 62
Bean Tacos 62
Bean Burros 63
Green Chile Chicken Burro 63
Red Chile Burros 64
Green Chile Burros 65
Fajita Marinade 66
Beef Fajitas 67
Mexican Stuffed Peppers 68
Green Chile Stew 69
Mexican Meatloaf 70
Mexican Lasagna 71
Mexican Turkey Lasagna 72
Black Bean & Brown Rice Burritos 73
Chalupa 74
Tamale Pie 74
Sloppy Jose's 75
Fiesta Chicken 75
Pescado Veracruz (Veracruz Fish) 76
Camarones Acapulco (Shrimp Acapulco Style) 76

Green Chile Sauce

This basic sauce can be used over many traditional Mexican dishes such as enchiladas, burros, tostadas and huevos rancheros. Green chile sauce is more perishable than red and should be made fresh.

1 lb. TOMATILLOS
8 fresh, roasted and peeled NEW MEXICO GREEN
 CHILES, chopped
1 lg. ONION, chopped
1-2 cloves GARLIC, chopped
1 can (15 oz.) FAT FREE CHICKEN BROTH
1/2 tsp. SALT
1/4 tsp. CUMIN
1/4 tsp. OREGANO

Husk and wash tomatillos. Slice into wedges. In a large saucepan combine tomatillos, chiles, onion, garlic, chicken broth and seasonings. Bring to a boil, reduce heat and simmer for 20 minutes. Pour into blender and pulse to desired consistency.

Makes approximately 4 cups.   Fat grams per serving = 0

Red Chile Sauce

8 lg. dried RED CHILE PODS
2 cloves GARLIC
1 med. ONION, chopped
WATER
2 Tbsp. FLOUR

2 cups WATER
1 tsp. OREGANO
1/4 tsp. CUMIN
SALT to taste

Wash chiles, remove stems and seeds (leave seeds for a hotter sauce). Place chiles, garlic and onion in a pot and cover with water. Bring to a boil, reduce heat and cook for 45 minutes. Drain water, place chiles, garlic, onion and flour in a blender and purée till smooth. Pour into saucepan, add 2 cups water and seasonings. Cook over medium heat, stirring constantly until sauce is thick and bubbly.

Makes 3 cups.   Fat grams per serving = 0

Muy Pronto Salsa Roja
(Quick Red Sauce)

3 Tbsp. FLOUR
1/4 cup WATER
2 cups WATER or FAT FREE CHICKEN BROTH
1/2 cup RED CHILE POWDER
1 tsp. GARLIC SALT
1/2 tsp. OREGANO
1/4 tsp. CUMIN

Mix flour and 1/4 cup water in saucepan, stirring until smooth. Add 2 cups broth, chile powder, garlic salt, oregano and cumin and cook over medium heat, stirring constantly, for 5 minutes or until thick and bubbly.

Makes 2 cups.   Fat grams per serving = 0

Bean Tostadas

12 CORN TORTILLAS
1 can (15 oz.) FAT FREE REFRIED BEANS
1/2 head LETTUCE, shredded
3/4 cup shredded LOW FAT CHEDDAR CHEESE
1 sm. ONION, diced
2 TOMATOES, diced
FAT FREE SOUR CREAM
SALSA

Toast tortillas until crisp in a hot, dry skillet (approximately 1-2 minutes per side.) Warm beans and spread on tortillas. Layer with lettuce, cheese, onion and tomatoes. Serve with sour cream and salsa.

Serves 6.   Fat grams per serving = 2

Beefy Tostadas

12 CORN TORTILLAS
1 lb. lean GROUND BEEF
1/2 tsp. GARLIC SALT
1/8 tsp. CUMIN
1/4 tsp. BLACK PEPPER
1 can (15 oz.) FAT FREE
    REFRIED BEANS

1/2 head LETTUCE, shredded
3/4 cup shredded LOW FAT
    CHEDDAR CHEESE
2 TOMATOES, diced
3 GREEN ONIONS, diced
FAT FREE SOUR CREAM
SALSA

Toast tortillas until crisp in a hot, dry skillet (approximately 1-2 minutes per side.) Brown ground beef, garlic salt, cumin and pepper in skillet. Drain thoroughly. Warm beans and spread on tortillas. Layer with beef, lettuce, cheese, tomatoes, onions and a dollop of sour cream. Add salsa to taste.

Serves 6.   Fat grams per serving = 9.8

Chicken Tostadas

4 skinless CHICKEN BREASTS
1 can (4 oz.) diced GREEN CHILES
1/4 tsp. GARLIC SALT
12 CORN TORTILLAS
1 can (15 oz.) FAT FREE
   REFRIED BEANS

1/2 head LETTUCE
3/4 cup shredded LOW FAT
   JACK CHEESE
2 TOMATOES, diced
FAT FREE SOUR CREAM
SALSA

Cover chicken breasts in water and boil until tender. Shred meat from bone with a fork and combine with green chiles and garlic salt. Toast tortillas until crisp in hot, dry skillet (approximately 1-2 minutes per side.) Warm beans and spread on tortillas. Add chicken and layer shredded lettuce, cheese and tomatoes. Serve with sour cream and salsa.

Serves 6.   Fat grams per serving = 4.4

Mexican Pizza

1 lb. lean GROUND BEEF
1 ONION, chopped
1/2 tsp. GARLIC SALT
1/2 tsp. OREGANO
1/4 tsp. CUMIN
4 (10-inch) FLOUR TORTILLAS
1 can (4 oz.) diced GREEN CHILES, drained
1/2 cup shredded LOW FAT JACK CHEESE
1/2 cup shredded LOW FAT CHEDDAR CHEESE
2 TOMATOES, chopped
1 bunch GREEN ONIONS, chopped
1 GREEN BELL PEPPER, diced
SALSA

Brown ground beef with onion in hot skillet. Drain thoroughly. Stir in garlic salt, oregano and cumin. Lay flour tortillas on cookie sheet(s). Slightly crisp tortillas in hot oven. Sprinkle tortillas with ground beef, green chiles, cheese, tomatoes, green onions and bell pepper. Put under broiler until cheese melts. Serve with salsa.

Serves 8.   Fat grams per serving = 9.6

Chicken Enchiladas

4 cups RED CHILE SAUCE (see page 55), heated
12 CORN TORTILLAS
2 cups shredded cooked CHICKEN BREASTS
1 1/2 cups shredded LOW FAT CHEDDAR CHEESE
1 lg. ONION, finely chopped
3 GREEN ONIONS, diced (for garnish)
FAT FREE SOUR CREAM   *Microwave tortillas for 1 min.*

Preheat oven to 325°. ~~Dip each tortilla in heated sauce.~~ Transfer tortillas to a large plate. On each tortilla, spread 2 tablespoons chicken, sprinkle with cheese and onion and roll up, placing seam side down in a shallow baking dish. Top enchiladas with remaining sauce, cheese and onion. Bake 20 minutes and garnish with green onions and sour cream.

Serves 6.   Fat grams per serving = 5.5

Beef Enchiladas

4 cups RED CHILE SAUCE
   (see page 55), heated
1 lb. lean GROUND BEEF
1/2 tsp. GARLIC SALT
1/2 tsp. OREGANO
1/4 tsp. PEPPER

12 CORN TORTILLAS
1 1/2 cups shredded LOW FAT
   CHEDDAR CHEESE
1 ONION, finely chopped
3 GREEN ONIONS, diced
1 TOMATO, diced

Preheat oven to 325°. Brown ground beef with seasonings. Drain thoroughly. Dip each tortilla in heated red chile sauce and transfer to a large plate. On each tortilla spread ground beef, cheese and onion. Roll up each tortilla and place seam side down in a shallow baking dish. Top with remaining sauce, cheese and onion. Bake 20 minutes and garnish with green onions and tomato.

Serves 6.   Fat grams per serving = 12.3

Cheese Enchiladas

4 cups RED CHILE SAUCE (see page 55), heated
12 CORN TORTILLAS
3/4 cup shredded LOW FAT CHEDDAR CHEESE
3/4 cup shredded LOW FAT JACK CHEESE
1 ONION, chopped
3 GREEN ONIONS, sliced (for garnish)
1 TOMATO, chopped
FAT FREE SOUR CREAM

Preheat oven to 325°. Dip each tortilla into sauce and transfer to platter. Place equal amounts of both cheeses on each tortilla and sprinkle with chopped onion. Roll and place seam side down in shallow baking dish. Top with remaining sauce and cheese. Bake for 25 minutes. To serve, garnish with green onions, tomatoes and dollops of sour cream.

Serves 6.   Fat grams per serving = 4.5

Chicken Enchilada Casserole

12 CORN TORTILLAS
6 skinless CHICKEN BREASTS, cooked
1 can (14.5 oz.) LOW FAT CREAM OF MUSHROOM SOUP
1 cup WATER
1 can (4 oz.) diced GREEN CHILES
1 ONION, finely chopped
3/4 cup shredded LOW FAT CHEDDAR CHEESE
3/4 cup shredded LOW FAT JACK CHEESE

Preheat oven to 325°. Cut tortillas into 1-inch strips and set aside. Shred chicken from bone and mix with soup, water, green chiles and onion. Line bottom of 9 x 13 baking dish with half of tortilla strips. Spread half of the chicken/soup mixture over the top. Sprinkle with half of the cheeses. Layer remaining tortilla strips and soup mixture and top with cheese. Bake uncovered for one hour. Before serving, garnish with sliced **GREEN ONIONS** and chopped **TOMATO**.

Serves 6.   Fat grams per serving = 6.5

Sonoran Enchiladas

These enchiladas differ from traditional enchiladas in that they are stacked instead of rolled.

2 cups RED CHILE SAUCE (see page 55)
12 CORN TORTILLAS
1 1/2 cups shredded LOW FAT CHEDDAR CHEESE
1 ONION, chopped
LETTUCE, shredded
2 TOMATOES, chopped
4 GREEN ONIONS, chopped
FAT FREE SOUR CREAM
SALSA

Heat red chile sauce thoroughly in a saucepan. Dip tortilla in sauce and lay flat on oven-proof platter or cookie sheet. Ladle 1 tablespoon of sauce over the tortilla and sprinkle cheese and chopped onion. Repeat this process to form a stack of three for each serving. Bake in 350° oven for 10 minutes. Remove to serving dish and garnish with lettuce, tomato and green onions. Serve with sour cream and salsa.

Serves 6. Fat grams per serving = 2.3

Variations: These enchiladas can be made with cooked shredded beef or chicken.

Taco Shells

12 CORN TORTILLAS

Drape tortillas over individual rungs on oven rack. Bake at 400° until crisp (approximately 5 minutes.) Carefully remove the taco shells and allow to cool.

Chicken Tacos

2 skinless CHICKEN BREASTS
GARLIC SALT
PEPPER
CHILI POWDER
8 TACO SHELLS
1/2 head LETTUCE, shredded
2 TOMATOES, chopped
1/2 cup shredded LOW FAT CHEDDAR CHEESE
SALSA

Arrange chicken breasts, flesh side up, on broiler pan and sprinkle with seasonings. Broil 3 to 5 minutes or until tender. Shred chicken from bone and place in taco shells. Fill each taco with lettuce, tomato and cheese. Serve with salsa.

Serves 4.   Fat grams per serving = 3.8

Beef Tacos

1 lb. lean GROUND BEEF
1 ONION, chopped
1/4 tsp. GARLIC SALT
1/4 tsp. CUMIN
1/2 tsp. CHILI POWDER
8 TACO SHELLS

1/2 head LETTUCE, shredded
1/2 cup shredded LOW FAT
   JACK CHEESE
2 TOMATOES, chopped
3 GREEN ONIONS, sliced
SALSA

Brown ground beef with onion in skillet. Drain thoroughly. Add seasonings. Fill each taco with meat, lettuce, cheese and tomatoes. Top with green onions and serve with salsa.

Serves 4.   Fat grams per serving = 14

Turkey Tacos

1 lb. GROUND TURKEY
1 ONION, chopped
1 can (4 oz.) diced GREEN
    CHILES
1/2 tsp. GARLIC SALT
1/4 tsp. PEPPER
1/4 tsp. CUMIN

8 TACO SHELLS
1/2 head LETTUCE, shredded
1/2 cup shredded LOW FAT
    CHEDDAR or JACK CHEESE
1 TOMATO, chopped
SALSA
FAT FREE SOUR CREAM

Brown ground turkey and onion in a skillet. Add green chiles, garlic salt, pepper and cumin. Spoon turkey into each taco shell. Layer lettuce, cheese and tomato. Serve with salsa and sour cream.

Serves 4.   Fat grams per serving = 13.5

Bean Tacos

This is a nice alternative to a meat taco.

1 can (15 oz.) FAT FREE REFRIED BEANS
1 can (15 oz.) FAT FREE BLACK BEANS, drained and rinsed
1 ONION, finely chopped
1 can (4 oz.) diced GREEN CHILES, drained
1/2 tsp. CHILI POWDER
1/4 tsp. GARLIC POWDER
12 TACO SHELLS
1 cup shredded LOW FAT
    CHEDDAR CHEESE
1/2 head LETTUCE, shredded
2 TOMATOES, chopped
SALSA

In a saucepan, combine beans, onion, chiles and seasonings. Heat thoroughly. Spoon bean mixture into taco shells. Sprinkle cheese, add lettuce and tomatoes. Top with salsa.

Serves 6.   Fat grams per serving = 3

Bean Burros

1 can (15 oz.) FAT FREE REFRIED BEANS
4 (12-inch) FLOUR TORTILLAS
1/2 ONION, finely chopped
3/4 cup shredded LOW FAT CHEDDAR CHEESE

Heat beans and spoon into warmed tortillas. Sprinkle with onions and cheese and roll up burro-style. Serve with **shredded LETTUCE, chopped TOMATO, and SALSA.**

Variation: For **Enchilada-Style,** place burro on oven-proof platter and ladle **Red Chile Sauce** (see page 55) over the top. Sprinkle with cheese and place under broiler for 1 minute.

Serves 4.   Fat grams per serving = 7.5

Green Chile Chicken Burro

2 cups cooked skinless CHICKEN BREAST, diced
1 can (4 oz.) diced GREEN CHILES
1 can (15 oz.) LOW FAT CREAM OF MUSHROOM SOUP
1/2 cup WATER
3 GREEN ONIONS, sliced
4 (12-inch) FLOUR TORTILLAS
3/4 cup shredded LOW FAT JACK CHEESE

In a saucepan, combine chicken, chiles, soup, water and green onions. Heat thoroughly and spoon into warmed flour tortillas. Sprinkle with cheese and roll burro-style. Serve with **shredded LETTUCE, chopped TOMATOES, FAT FREE SOUR CREAM** and **SALSA.**

Serves 4.   Fat grams per serving = 9.7

Red Chile Burros

1 1/2 lbs. lean CHUCK ROAST
WATER
1 sm. ONION, chopped
2 cloves GARLIC, minced
1/4 tsp. OREGANO
1 1/2 cups RED CHILE SAUCE (see page 55)
6 (12-inch) FLOUR TORTILLAS
shredded LETTUCE
chopped TOMATOES
1/2 cup shredded LOW FAT CHEDDAR CHEESE
FAT FREE SOUR CREAM (optional)
SALSA

Remove all visible signs of fat from chuck roast and place in cooking pot and cover with water.

Bring to a boil, reduce heat and cover and simmer until meat is fully cooked. Let cool and cut into bite-size pieces or shred with a fork. In a large nonstick skillet, sauté meat with onion, garlic and oregano. Add red chile sauce and heat thoroughly. Spoon into flour tortillas and roll burro-style. Garnish with lettuce, tomatoes, cheese, sour cream and salsa.

Serves 6.   Fat grams per serving = 10

Green Chile Burros

1 1/2 lbs. lean CHUCK ROAST
WATER
1 ONION, chopped
1 GREEN BELL PEPPER, chopped
1 can (4 oz.) diced GREEN CHILES
1/2 tsp. GARLIC SALT
1/8 tsp. CUMIN
1/8 tsp. OREGANO
6 (12-inch) FLOUR TORTILLAS
1/2 head LETTUCE, shredded
1 TOMATO, chopped
SALSA

Remove all visible signs of fat from chuck roast and place in cooking pot and cover with water. Stew until fully cooked. Allow meat to cool and shred. In a large nonstick skillet, add shredded chuck roast, onion and bell pepper. Sauté until onion and pepper are tender, stirring constantly. Reduce heat, add green chiles and seasonings. Stir and cover and allow to simmer for 10 minutes. Spoon meat into warmed flour tortillas and roll burro-style. Garnish with lettuce and tomato. Serve with salsa.

Serves 6.   Fat grams per serving = 8.5

Variation: For **Enchilada-Style** place burro on oven-proof platter and ladle *Green Chile Sauce* (see page 54) over top. Sprinkle with shredded **LOW FAT CHEDDAR CHEESE** and place under broiler for 1 minute. Serve with **FAT FREE SOUR CREAM.**

*The best way to serve **fajitas** is to grill onions, tomatoes, and bell peppers and present along with your choice of cooked meat(s) on a sizzling platter accompanied by warmed flour tortillas and your favorite garnishes.*

Fajita Marinade

1/2 cup WATER
1/4 cup LEMON JUICE
2 cloves GARLIC, crushed
1 Tbsp. WORCESTERSHIRE SAUCE
1/2 tsp. OREGANO
1/2 tsp. CUMIN
2 tsp. BROWN SUGAR
dash of TABASCO®
1/8 tsp. LIQUID SMOKE

Combine all ingredients in a glass bowl and blend well. Marinate meat or vegetables, in the refrigerator, for at least one hour before cooking. When using tougher cuts of meat marinate for a longer period of time, 2-4 hours.

Fat grams per serving = 0

Beef Fajitas

1 lb. FLANK STEAK
FAJITA MARINADE (see page 66)
1 GREEN BELL PEPPER, cut into strips
1 ONION, cut into wedges
1 TOMATO, cut into wedges

Remove all visible fat from flank steak. Place steak in shallow baking dish or place in a locking plastic bag. Pour marinade over flank steak and refrigerate for 4 hours. Cut steak into thin strips and place in hot nonstick skillet. Just before meat is done add vegetables and continue cooking until desired tenderness. Serve with warmed **FLOUR** or **CORN TORTILLAS.** Accompany with plenty of **shredded LETTUCE, chopped TOMATOES, FAT FREE SOUR CREAM, SALSA,** *Pico de Gallo* (see page 19), and *Frijoles* (see page 42.)

Serves 8.   Fat grams per serving = 4

Variations: Substitute skinless **CHICKEN BREASTS** or **SHRIMP** for flank steak. For a meatless meal try a variety of marinated and grilled vegetables such as **ZUCCHINI, CAULIFLOWER, BROCCOLI, ONIONS, BELL PEPPERS, CARROTS** and **POTATOES.**

Mexican Stuffed Peppers

8 lg. GREEN or RED BELL PEPPERS
1/2 lb. GROUND TURKEY
1 1/2 cups cooked RICE
1 TOMATO, finely diced
2 GREEN ONIONS, finely chopped
1 can (4 oz.) diced GREEN CHILES
1/2 tsp. GARLIC SALT
1/4 tsp. PEPPER
1/2 tsp. OREGANO
3 Tbsp. SALSA
1 EGG, slightly beaten
1 can (8 oz.) TOMATO SAUCE

Try to choose block-shaped bell peppers so they will stand in baking dish. Wash, core, and seed bell peppers. Set in baking dish. Brown ground turkey, stirring to crumble. Remove from heat and place in large bowl. Add cooked rice, tomato, onions, green chiles, seasonings, salsa and egg. Blend well and fill each pepper with turkey/rice mixture. Pour tomato sauce over peppers and bake in a pre-heated 350° oven for 45 minutes.

Serves 8.   Fat grams per serving = 3.6

Green Chile Stew

*This satisfying stew will warm your soul on a
cold winter day.*

2 lbs. lean CHUCK ROAST, cubed
1 ONION, chopped
1 GREEN or RED BELL PEPPER, chopped
1 clove GARLIC, crushed
1 Tbsp. VEGETABLE OIL
3 CARROTS, sliced
3 POTATOES, cubed
1 can (15 oz.) STEWED TOMATOES
1 can (15 oz.) PINTO BEANS
1 can (7 oz.) diced GREEN CHILES
2 cups WATER
2 cups GREEN CHILE SAUCE (see page 54)
SALT and PEPPER to taste

Remove all visible signs of fat from beef. In large pot, brown
meat, onion, pepper and garlic in oil. Add remaining ingredients and bring mixture to a boil. Reduce heat, cover and simmer
for 1 1/2 hours. Serve with warmed **FLOUR TORTILLAS.**

Serves 6.   Fat grams per serving = 8.3

Variation: Substitute **PORK** for beef or a combination of the two.

Mexican Meatloaf

Try this spicy twist to an old favorite.

2 lbs. GROUND TURKEY
1 cup crushed BAKED TORTILLA CHIPS
1/2 sm. ONION, chopped
1 can (4 oz.) diced GREEN CHILES
3 Tbsp. SALSA
1/2 tsp. OREGANO
1/2 tsp. CHILI POWDER
1/2 tsp. GARLIC SALT
1/4 tsp. CAYENNE
1/4 tsp. CUMIN
1 can (8 oz.) TOMATO SAUCE

Preheat oven to 350°. In large mixing bowl, combine all ingredients except for tomato sauce. Form into loaf (in shallow baking dish) or press lightly into a 9 x 5 loaf pan. Bake for 1 hour. In last 10 minutes of baking time pour tomato sauce over top. Remove from oven and allow to set for 5-10 minutes before slicing.

Serves 8.   Fat grams per serving = 11.25

Mexican Lasagna

Sauce:
- 1 Tbsp. OLIVE OIL
- 1 GREEN BELL PEPPER, diced
- 1 ONION, chopped
- 3 cloves GARLIC, crushed
- 1 can (7 oz.) diced GREEN CHILES
- 1 jar (16 oz.) SALSA
- 1 can (16 oz.) stewed TOMATOES, chopped
- 1 can (8 oz.) TOMATO SAUCE
- 1/2 tsp. OREGANO
- 1/2 tsp. CUMIN
- 1/2 tsp. PEPPER

Heat oil in a large skillet and sauté bell pepper, onion and garlic until tender. Add green chiles, salsa, tomatoes, tomato sauce and seasonings. Simmer for 20 minutes.

Cheese Filling:
- 1 ctn. (16 oz.) FAT FREE COTTAGE CHEESE
- 1 cup FAT FREE RICOTTA CHEESE
- 1 can (4 oz.) diced GREEN CHILES
- 2 EGG WHITES
- 1/2 tsp. OREGANO
- 1/4 cup chopped fresh CILANTRO

Combine cottage and ricotta cheeses with chiles, egg whites, oregano and cilantro.

12 CORN TORTILLAS, torn in half
1 cup shredded LOW FAT JACK CHEESE

Spoon 1/3 of the sauce in a 9 x 13 baking dish. Cover with half the tortilla pieces and spread half of the cheese filling over the tortillas. Spoon 1/3 of tomato sauce over the cheese filling and sprinkle with 1/2 cup jack cheese. Layer remaining tortilla pieces, cheese filling and remaining sauce. Top with jack cheese. Bake at 350° for one hour. Let stand 10 minutes before serving. Garnish with fresh **TOMATOES** and **sprigs of CILANTRO**.

Serves 10.   Fat grams per serving = 3.2

Mexican Turkey Lasagna

1 lb. ground TURKEY
1 ONION, chopped
1 can (15 oz.) STEWED TOMATOES, cut up
1/2 cup SALSA
1 can (8 oz.) TOMATO SAUCE
1 cup WATER
2 Tbsp. CHILI POWDER
1/2 tsp. GARLIC SALT
1 cup FAT FREE COTTAGE CHEESE
1 cup FAT FREE SOUR CREAM
12 CORN TORTILLAS
1 1/2 cups shredded LOW FAT JACK CHEESE

In a large skillet, brown turkey with onion. Stir in tomatoes, salsa, tomato sauce, water and seasonings. Simmer for 20 minutes. Combine cottage cheese and sour cream together. Spoon 1/4 of the tomato sauce mixture in the bottom of a 9 x 13 baking dish. Arrange 4 of the tortillas over the sauce. Spread 1/3 of the cottage cheese and sour cream over the tortillas and sprinkle with 1/3 of the jack cheese. Repeat two more layers ending with the cheese on top. Bake for 30 minutes in a 325° oven. Allow to set for 10 minutes before serving.

Serves 8.   Fat grams per serving = 9

Black Bean &
Brown Rice Burritos

Healthy and nutritious, this delicious combination is sure to become one of your favorites!

1 can (15 oz.) **FAT FREE BLACK BEANS**, drained and rinsed
1 lg. **ONION**, finely grated
1 can (4 oz.) diced **GREEN CHILES**
2 Tbsp. chopped fresh **CILANTRO**
1 tsp. **RED CHILI POWDER**
8 **WHOLE WHEAT FLOUR TORTILLAS**
2 cups cooked **BROWN RICE**
1 cup **SALSA**

Preheat oven to 350°. In a large mixing bowl, mash beans with grated onion. Stir in chiles, cilantro and chili powder. Spread tortillas out on a counter and place equal amounts of the bean mixture on each one. Top with a 1/4 cup of cooked brown rice. Fold in sides and roll tortilla to completely enclose contents. Place all eight burritos, seam side down, in a nonstick baking pan. Pour salsa evenly over the burritos and bake at 350° for 20 minutes. Garnish with **shredded LOW FAT CHEESE** and **FAT FREE SOUR CREAM.**

Serves 8.   Fat grams per serving = 3.5

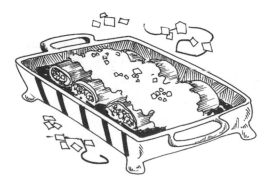

Chalupa

This tasty combination is great for tostadas and burros!

3 lbs. PORK ROAST, trimmed of all fat
1 lb. PINTO BEANS, washed
2 GARLIC CLOVES, chopped
1 can (7 oz.) diced GREEN CHILES
3 Tbsp. CHILI POWDER
1 Tbsp. CUMIN
1 Tbsp. OREGANO
1 Tbsp. SALT

Place all ingredients in a large pot, kettle or crock pot and cover with water. Simmer over low heat, adding water if needed. After 6 hours, remove bones and break up roast. Continue cooking with lid off until thick. Serve on **TOSTADA SHELLS** or **TORTILLAS (burro-style)** with **shredded LETTUCE, chopped TOMATOES** and **ONIONS**. Chalupa freezes perfectly!

Serves 12.   Fat grams per serving = 4.3

Tamale Pie

1 lb. GROUND TURKEY
3/4 cup CORNMEAL
1 EGG
1 1/2 cups SKIM MILK
1 Tbsp. CHILI POWDER
1/2 tsp. GARLIC SALT
1/4 tsp. CUMIN
1/4 tsp. CAYENNE

1 can (15 oz.) WHOLE KERNEL CORN, drained
1 can (15 oz.) STEWED TOMATOES, cut up
4 GREEN ONIONS, chopped
3/4 cup shredded LOW FAT CHEDDAR CHEESE

Brown ground turkey in a nonstick skillet until crumbly. In a large bowl, combine cornmeal, egg and milk. Add seasonings, corn, tomatoes, green onion and cooked turkey. When thoroughly mixed, pour into a lightly oiled casserole dish. Sprinkle cheese over the top. Cover and bake at 325° for 45 minutes.

Serves 6-8.   Fat grams per serving = 8.5

Sloppy Jose's

1 lb. GROUND TURKEY
1 ONION, chopped
1 GREEN BELL PEPPER, chopped
1 clove GARLIC, crushed
1 can (4 oz.) diced GREEN CHILES
2 cups cooked, or canned, PINTO BEANS
1 can (8 oz.) TOMATO SAUCE
1 Tbsp. CHILI POWDER
1/2 tsp. OREGANO
SALT and PEPPER to taste

In a nonstick skillet, sauté turkey, onion, bell pepper and garlic until turkey is browned. Add remaining ingredients and simmer for 30 minutes. Serve over split hamburger buns, cornbread or warmed tortillas.

Serves 8.   Fat grams per serving = 5.6

Fiesta Chicken

4 CHICKEN BREASTS, boned and skinned
1/2 tsp. GARLIC SALT
1/2 tsp. CUMIN
PEPPER to taste
1 can (4 oz.) diced GREEN CHILES
1 cup CORN
1 can (15 oz.) FAT FREE BLACK BEANS, drained and rinsed
1 cup SALSA
fresh CILANTRO

Season chicken breasts with garlic salt, cumin and pepper. Brown on both sides in a nonstick skillet. Add green chiles, corn, black beans and salsa. Cover and simmer for 15 minutes. Garnish with fresh cilantro. Serve with rice.

Serves 4.   Fat grams per serving = 3.3

Pescado Veracruz

(Veracruz Fish)

1 1/2 lbs. RED SNAPPER FILLETS
1/2 LIME
1 med. ONION, thinly sliced
1 clove GARLIC, minced
2 JALAPEÑOS, seeded and sliced
1/2 Tbsp. VEGETABLE OIL
3 TOMATOES, cut into large chunks
TABASCO®

Squeeze lime juice over fish fillets and set aside. In a large nonstick skillet sauté onion, garlic and jalapeños in vegetable oil. Add tomatoes and a dash of Tabasco and simmer, uncovered, for 5 minutes. Place fish on top of mixture and spoon sauce over fish. Cover and simmer for 5-7 minutes, or until fish flakes when tested with a fork. Remove fish to serving platter and spoon sauce over each fillet.

Serves 4.   Fat grams per serving = 4

Camarones Acapulco

(Shrimp Acapulco Style)

*This cold dish is best when accompanied with a vegetable salad, warm quesadillas and hot **Spanish Rice** (see page 42.)*

2 lbs. cooked SHRIMP, shelled and deveined, with tails intact
1 cup HOT SAUCE
3 Tbsp. HORSERADISH
2 Tbsp. fresh LEMON JUICE
1/2 tsp. CHILI POWDER
TABASCO®

Chill shrimp in refrigerator. In a small bowl blend hot sauce, horseradish, lemon juice, chili powder and a dash of Tabasco until smooth. Chill sauce and serve with shrimp.

Serves 6.   Fat grams per serving = <1

Desserts

Arroz Dulce (Rice Pudding) 78

Capirotada (Bread Pudding) 78

Meringues de Chocolate (Chocolate Meringues) 79

Meringues de Almendra (Almond Meringues) 79

Flan (Custard) with Flan Sauce 80

Pastel de Piña (Pineapple Cake) 81

     and Cream Cheese Icing 81

Sweet Tortilla Roll-ups 81

Pastel Coctel de Fruta (Fruit Cocktail Cake) 82

Gelatina de Yogurt con Fresas

     (Yogurt-Strawberry Gelatin) 82

Arroz Dulce
(Rice Pudding)

1/2 cup **SKIM MILK**
1/2 cup **RAISINS**
3 cups cooked long-grain **WHITE RICE**
1 can (14 oz.) **NON-FAT SWEETENED CONDENSED MILK**
1/2 tsp. **VANILLA**
1/2 tsp. **CINNAMON**
1/4 tsp. **NUTMEG**

Combine all ingredients in a saucepan and stir over medium heat until mixture is thick. Serve warm or chill in refrigerator for 1 hour. To serve, place in individual serving bowls and sprinkle with additional nutmeg.

Serves 6.   Fat grams per serving = <1

Capirotada
(Bread Pudding)

1 cup **RAISINS**
1 cup **ORANGE JUICE**
1/2 tsp. **CINNAMON**
1/2 tsp. **ALLSPICE**
1/2 tsp. grated **ORANGE PEEL**
3/4 cup **BROWN SUGAR**

1/2 tsp. **VANILLA**
10 slices **BREAD**
2 cups shredded **LOW FAT JACK CHEESE**
1 **APPLE**, peeled, cored and diced

Combine raisins, orange juice, cinnamon, allspice, orange peel, brown sugar and vanilla in a saucepan and bring to a boil, stirring constantly. Toast bread and cut into cubes. Place bread cubes in a large bowl and toss with raisin mixture. Add 1 1/2 cups cheese and apple and mix together. Turn into a lightly oiled baking dish and sprinkle with remaining cheese. Bake in a preheated 375° oven for 15 minutes. Serve warm with maple or brown sugar syrup.

Serves 10.   Fat grams per serving = 4.6

Meringues de Chocolate
(Chocolate Meringues)

Meringues are placed in the oven to dry rather than bake. It is important not to remove them before they have completely cooled inside the oven.

4 EGG WHITES	2 Tbsp. COCOA
1 cup SUGAR	1/2 tsp. VANILLA

Preheat oven to 225°. Line a cookie sheet with parchment paper. Beat egg whites until stiff. Add sugar a little at a time, continuing to beat until glossy. Dissolve cocoa in a small amount of water and add vanilla. Fold into egg whites. Drop by teaspoonfuls onto cookie sheet, leaving 1 inch between meringues. Place in oven for 1 hour, or until firm to the touch. Cool in oven before removing.

Makes 12 meringues.   Fat grams per serving = 0

Meringues de Almendra
(Almond Meringues)

4 EGG WHITES	1 cup SUGAR
1/8 tsp. CREAM OF TARTAR	1 tsp. ALMOND EXTRACT

Preheat oven to 225°. Line a cookie sheet with parchment paper. Beat egg whites until frothy. Add cream of tartar and almond extract and continue beating. Add sugar, 1 teaspoon at a time until egg whites are stiff and glossy. Drop by teaspoonfuls onto cookie sheet, leaving 1 inch between meringues. Place in oven for 1 hour, or until meringues are firm to the touch. Leave in oven to cool completely. Meringues can be stored tightly covered until ready to use.

Makes 12 meringues.   Fat grams per serving = 0

Flan
(Custard)

A popular traditional Mexican dessert.

3 EGGS, slightly beaten
1/4 tsp. SALT
1 can (14 oz.) NON-FAT SWEETENED CONDENSED MILK
1 1/2 cups SKIM MILK
1/2 Tbsp. VANILLA
NUTMEG

In a bowl, combine eggs, salt and sweetened condensed milk. Add skim milk slowly, stirring constantly. Add vanilla and blend well. Preheat oven to 350°. Pour custard into 6 custard dishes. Sprinkle each with nutmeg. Place custard cups in baking pan, add hot water to the pan 2/3 of the way up the sides of the custard cups. Bake for 30-35 minutes. To test for doneness, knife should come out clean when inserted into center. Refrigerate for several hours. The longer it is chilled, the firmer it becomes. To serve, top with **Flan Sauce.**

Serves 6. 　　　　　　　　　　　Fat grams per serving = 2

Flan Sauce

6 Tbsp. BROWN SUGAR
1/2 cup WATER
1/2 tsp. CINNAMON

In a saucepan dissolve sugar by adding water slowly. Add cinnamon. Heat until smooth, clear syrup forms. Serve over flan.

Pastel de Piña
(Pineapple Cake)

2 cups SUGAR
2 cups FLOUR
2 tsp. BAKING SODA
2 EGGS
1 can (20 oz.) crushed PINEAPPLE, undrained
1 tsp. VANILLA

Preheat oven to 325°. Lightly oil a 9 x 13 baking dish. Combine all ingredients in mixing bowl and blend thoroughly. Pour into baking dish and bake for 35-40 minutes, or until tester comes out clean. Top immediately with ***Cream Cheese Icing.***

Serves 12.   Fat grams per serving = <1

Cream Cheese Icing

2 cups sifted POWDERED SUGAR
1 pkg. (8 oz.) FAT FREE CREAM CHEESE, room temperature
2 Tbsp. SKIM MILK

Blend all ingredients until smooth. Spread on pineapple cake.

Sweet Tortilla Roll-ups

1/2 cup FAT FREE RICOTTA CHEESE
2 Tbsp. SUGAR
2 tsp. CINNAMON
1/4 tsp. VANILLA
4 (10-inch) FLOUR TORTILLAS

Set oven to broil. In a mixing bowl blend ricotta cheese, sugar, cinnamon and vanilla. Spread about 2 tablespoons of ricotta down center of each tortilla. Fold ends of each tortilla in and roll up like a burrito. Place on cookie sheet and broil for approximately 1 minute. Serve warm.

Serves 4.   Fat grams per serving = 3

Pastel Coctel de Fruta
(Fruit Cocktail Cake)

2 cups FLOUR
1 1/2 cups SUGAR
2 tsp. BAKING SODA
1 tsp. SALT
1 CAN (28 OZ.) FRUIT COCKTAIL, undrained
1/2 cup RAISINS
2 EGGS
2 tsp. VANILLA
3/4 cup POWDERED SUGAR

Preheat oven to 350°. Lightly oil a 9 x 13 baking pan. In a large mixing bowl sift flour, sugar, baking soda and salt. Add fruit cocktail, with juice, and raisins. In a small bowl lightly beat eggs and add vanilla. Combine with flour mixture. Pour into baking pan and bake for 45 minutes or until done. Before slicing, sprinkle with powdered sugar.

Serves 10.   Fat grams per serving = <1

Gelatina de Yogurt con Fresas
(Yogurt-Strawberry Gelatin)

1 pkg. (6 oz.) STRAWBERRY GELATIN
2 cups boiling WATER
2 cups FAT FREE STRAWBERRY YOGURT
2 cups sliced STRAWBERRIES

Dissolve gelatin in boiling water. Allow to cool for 10 minutes. Stir in yogurt and strawberries. Pour into decorative mold. Refrigerate for at least 4 hours. Unmold and serve.

Serves 8.   Fat grams per serving = 0

Beverages

Traditional Margarita 84

Margarita Punch 84

Sangrita 85

Tequila Sunrise 85

Sangria 86

Refresco de Fresas 86

Mexican Hot Chocolate 87

Mexican Mocha...87

Café de Almendra (Almond Coffee) 88

Café Mexicano (Mexican Coffee)...........................88

Traditional Margarita

4 oz. TEQUILA
2 oz. TRIPLE SEC®
2 cups LEMON-LIME MIX
ICE, crushed
LEMON or LIME wedges
COARSE SALT

Combine tequila, Triple Sec and lemon-lime mix in a cocktail shaker. Add ice and shake well. Rub lemon or lime wedge around rims of two glasses and dip rims into salt. Strain the margaritas into glasses from shaker.

Serves 2.   Fat grams per serving = 0

Margarita Punch

1 can (6 oz.) frozen LIMEADE concentrate
1 can (6 oz.) frozen LEMONADE concentrate
4 cups crushed ICE
1/2 cup POWDERED SUGAR
1 bottle (2-liter) GINGER ALE or CLUB SODA, chilled
2 cups TEQUILA
LIME wedges
COARSE SALT

In a blender combine limeade, lemonade, ice and powdered sugar. Blend until slushy. Pour into punch bowl and stir in ginger ale and tequila. When ready to serve rub glass rims with lime wedges and dip glasses in salt (if desired).

Serves 16.   Fat grams per serving = 0

Sangrita

3 cups V-8® JUICE
1/2 cup ORANGE JUICE
2 Tbsp. LIME JUICE
2 oz. diced GREEN CHILES
1 Tbsp. SUGAR
1 tsp. WORCESTERSHIRE SAUCE
TABASCO® to taste
1/4 tsp. ONION POWDER

Combine all ingredients in blender and blend until smooth. Chill and serve in tall glasses over ice. Garnish with **CELERY STALK** in each glass.

Serves 6.   Fat grams per serving = 0

Tequila Sunrise

2 oz. TEQUILA
1/2 cup ORANGE JUICE
1 Tbsp. GRENADINE
1 tsp. LIME JUICE
ICE, crushed
MARASCHINO CHERRY

Combine tequila, orange juice, grenadine and lime juice in blender and blend. Pour into tall glass over crushed ice. Garnish with cherry.

Serves 1.   Fat grams per serving = 0

Sangria

A red wine punch of Spanish origin.

1 cup SUGAR
4 cups WATER
4 cups ORANGE JUICE
4 cups RED WINE
1 cup BRANDY
1 ORANGE, sliced
crushed ICE

In a large punch bowl dissolve sugar in water. Add juice, wine and brandy. Cover and chill. Before serving, float orange slices on top. Pour over crushed ice in tall glasses.

Serves 12.   Fat grams per serving = 0

Refresco de Fresas

(Strawberry Drink)

1 basket STRAWBERRIES (hulled and sliced)
6 cups WATER
1/2 cup SUGAR
crushed ICE

Combine strawberries and 2 cups water in blender and purée. Add remaining water and sugar and mix thoroughly. Cover and refrigerate. To serve, pour over crushed ice in tall glasses. If desired, garnish with **MINT sprigs.**

Serves 6   Fat grams per serving = 0

Mexican Hot Chocolate

1/2 cup COCOA POWDER
1/2 cup MASA HARINA
6 cups SKIM MILK
1 tsp. VANILLA
1 cup SUGAR
6 CINNAMON STICKS

In a large saucepan combine cocoa, masa harina, skim milk, vanilla and sugar and blend well. Simmer over medium heat, stirring constantly until thickened. Pour into mugs and serve with cinnamon sticks.

Serves 6.   Fat grams per serving = 5.8

Mexican Mocha

4 cups COFFEE (instant or brewed)
2 cups SKIM MILK
1/2 cup COCOA POWDER
2 Tbsp. SUGAR
1/2 tsp. VANILLA
1/4 tsp. CINNAMON

In a large saucepan combine coffee, milk, cocoa powder and sugar and bring to a boil. Remove from heat and add cinnamon and vanilla. Pour into a blender and process on high until frothy. Serve hot.

Serves 6.   Fat grams per serving = <1

Café de Almendra
(Almond Coffee)

1 cup hot COFFEE
1 oz. AMARETTO
4 oz. FAT FREE VANILLA ICE CREAM
CINNAMON

In a large coffee mug combine coffee and amaretto. Spoon in ice cream and sprinkle with cinnamon.

Serves 1.   Fat grams per serving = 0

Café Mexicano
(Mexican Coffee)

1 cup hot COFFEE
1 oz. KAHLUA
1/2 oz. TEQUILA
1 tsp. BROWN SUGAR
CINNAMON

In a large coffee mug combine all ingredients.

Serves 1.   Fat grams per serving = 0

Chile Glossary

Chile vs. chili: In this book, chile refers to the actual peppers and chili refers to a prepared dish typically consisting of chile peppers with meat.

Anaheim: Also called "California" or "California green chiles". These are mild long chiles which are closely related to the *New Mexico chile*. These chiles are great for stuffing *(rellenos)* and can be used to make a mild green sauce with tomatillos. The red, dried form is most often seen hanging in "ristras." The red is sweeter than the green.

Ancho: A dried *poblano* chile. The most commonly used dried chile in Mexico. It is a very dark red (almost black) when dried. Used in tamales, menudo and many sauces.

Cayenne: Used most often in powdered form as a seasoning. Usually 2-4 inches long, bright red and tapering to a point. Very hot.

Chiltepin: A wild form of the *pequín*. Medium red, oval-shaped and about the size of a marble. This dried chile is very hot.

Chipotle: A large, dried, smoked jalapeño. The flavor is smoky, pungent and very hot.

Habanero: The hottest chile in the world! This lantern-shaped, 2-inch long chile ranges from dark green to orange-red to red in color. It is used in salsas, chutneys and marinades and is sometimes pickled.

Jalapeño: Bright medium to dark green, about 2-3 inches long, tapering to a rounded end. The most popular hot chile in the United States. Can be eaten raw, pickled, roasted and is available canned.

New Mexico: Slightly hotter than the *Anaheim chile*, utilized the same way. The dried red chiles can be seen hanging in "ristras" throughout the Southwest.

Pasilla: Also called *chile negro* is a dried *chilaca chile*. Dark brown, wrinkled, tapered, and about 5-6 inches long. Used in making sauces.

Poblano: One of the most popular fresh chiles in Mexico. These chiles are triangular in shape, dark green, about 4-5 inches long and 2-3 inches in diameter. Used cooked or roasted. Excellent for *chiles rellenos.*

Serrano: The hottest chile commonly available in the U.S. This smooth-skinned green and red chile is used in sauces and salsas.

Tabasco: Bright orange-red, about 1 1/2 inches long. Very hot. Used primarily in Tabasco® sauces.

Index

Albondigas Soup   34
alfalfa sprouts   26
Appetizers
    Avocado Dip   18
    Baked Fiesta Dip   20
    Basic Salsa   9
    Black Bean Dip   12
    Chef's Choice Bean Dip   13
    Chunky Bean Dip   13
    Cilantro Salsa   10
    Corn Crisps   17
    Creamy Pinto Bean Dip   12
    Fiery Salsa   9
    Layered Dip   20
    Low Fat Corn Tortilla Chips   8
    Low Fat Flour Tortilla Chips   8
    Nachos   19
    Pickled Potatoes   14
    Pico de Gallo   19
    Quick Salsa   10
    Salsa Blanca   18
    Salsa Picante   11
    Salsa Verde   11
    Spicy Jicama Sticks   14
    Spicy Medley   15
    Stuffed Green Chiles   15
    Tortilla Roll-ups   16
    Tuna-stuffed Jalapeños   16
    Veggie Quesadillas   17
Arroz de Mexico   51
Arroz Dulce   78
avocado   18
Avocado Dip   18
Baked Chile Relleno   24
Baked Fiesta Dip   20
Basic Salsa   9
Bean Burros   63
Bean Dips   12-13
Bean Tacos   62
Bean Tostadas   56
beans
    black 12-13, 30, 37, 39, 48, 62, 73, 75
    garbanzo   13, 37
    kidney   13, 35, 37
    navy 13
    pinto 12-13, 23, 29-30, 42, 48-49, 69, 74-75
    refried   20, 56-57, 62-63
Beef Enchiladas   58
Beef Fajitas   67
Beef Tacos   61
Beefy Tostadas   56
bell peppers
    green 11, 19-20, 28, 33, 36, 38-39, 42, 49, 51-52, 57, 65, 67-69, 71, 75
    red 30, 38, 51, 67-69
    yellow 38, 67
Beverages
    Café de Almendra   88
    Café Mexicano   88
    Margarita Punch   84
    Mexican Hot Chocolate   87
    Mexican Mocha   87
    Refresco de Fresas   86
    Sangria   86
    Sangrita   85
    Tequila Sunrise   85
    Traditional Margarita   84
Black Bean & Brown Rice Burritos   73
Black Bean & Rice Soup   30
Black Bean Dip   12
Black Bean Salad   39
Black Beans & Corn   48
Border Pasta   45
Breakfasts
    Baked Chile Relleno   24
    Breakfast Burritos   26
    Corn Pudding   25
    Huevos con Chiles Verde   22
    Huevos Rancheros   23
    Low Fat Chorizo   23
    Mission Burritos   26
    Torta de Chile Verde   25
Breakfast Burritos   26
broccoli   67
broth, chicken 30, 32, 34, 51

Café de Almendra 88
Café Mexicano 88
Calabacitas 43
Calabacitas con Jamón 43
Caldo de Pollo 31
Camarones Acapulco 76
Capirotada 78
carrots 15, 28, 30-31, 34-35, 38, 51, 67, 69
cauliflower 15, 67
celery 13, 28, 30,-31, 33-35, 37-38, 48
Chalupa 74
Cheese Enchiladas 59
Chef's Choice Bean Dip 13
Chicken Enchilada Casserole 59
Chicken Enchiladas 58
Chicken Taco Salad 37
Chicken Tacos 61
Chicken Tostadas 57
Chile Cornbread 46
Chile Rice 45
chiles
    Anaheim 11, 31
    chiltepin 11, 23
    green 9-10, 13, 15-20, 22, 24, 26, 28,
        30, 33, 38-39, 43-47, 49-50, 57, 59,
        62-63, 65, 68-71, 73-75, 85
    jalapeños 9, 14-16, 19-20, 29, 38, 47,
        76
    New Mexico 31, 54
    red 55
    yellow 11
Chili Colorado 51
Chunky Bean Dip 13
Cilantro Salsa 10
corn 39, 43, 46, 48, 75
Corn Crisps 17
Corn Pudding 25
Corn Salad 39
Creamy Pinto Bean Dip 12
cucumbers 13, 28, 36-38
dairy
    fat free
        cottage cheese 18, 20, 49-50, 71-72
        cream cheese 12, 15-16, 45, 81
        mayonnaise 38, 48
        ricotta cheese 71, 81

sour cream 16-18, 20, 35, 38, 40,
    44-46, 49, 56-59, 60, 62, 64-65, 67,
    72-73
strawberry yogurt 82
vanilla ice cream 88
low fat
    cheddar cheese 17, 19-20, 23-24,
        26, 33, 37, 45-46,50, 56-65, 73-74
    jack cheese 20, 24, 28, 35, 40, 43,
        57, 59, 61-63, 71-72
Desserts
    Arroz Dulce 78
    Capirotada 78
    Flan 80
    Gelatina de Yogurt con Fresas 82
    Meringues de Almendra 79
    Meringues de Chocolate 79
    Pastel Coctel de Fruta 82
    Pastel de Piña 81
    Sweet Tortilla Roll-ups 81
eggs 23, 25, 46, 68, 74, 80-82
    substitute 22, 24, 26
    whites 71, 79
Ensalada de Pepiño 36
Ensalada de Tres Frijoles 37
Fajita Marinade 66
Fiery Salsa 9
Fiesta Chicken 75
Fiesta Hominy 52
Fiesta Salad 38
Flan 80
Frijoles 42
Frijoles del Mar 48
fruits
    apple 78
    fruit cocktail 82
    orange 86
    pineapple 44, 81
    raisins 78, 82
    strawberries 82, 86
Gazpacho 28
Gelatina de Yogurt con Fresas 82
Green Chile Burros 65
Green Chile Chicken Burro 63
Green Chile Mashed Potatoes 44
Green Chile Sauce 54

Hearty Bean Soup   30
hominy   32, 46, 52
Hominy con Chile   46
Huevos con Chiles Verde   22
Huevos Rancheros   23
jicama   14-15, 36
Jicama Salad   36
Layered Dip   20
Lemon Rice   52
liquor/liqueurs/wines
   amaretto   88
   brandy   86
   grenadine   85
   kahlua   88
   red wine   86
   tequila   85, 88
   Triple Sec®   84
Low Fat Chorizo   23
Low Fat Corn Tortilla Chips   8
Low Fat Flour Tortilla Chips   8
Margarita Punch   84
Main Dishes
   Bean Burros   63
   Bean Tacos   62
   Bean Tostadas   56
   Beef Enchiladas   58
   Beef Fajitas   67
   Beef Tacos   60
   Beefy Tostadas   56
   Black Bean & Brown Rice Burritos   73
   Camarones Acapulco   76
   Chalupa   74
   Cheese Enchiladas   59
   Chicken Enchilada Casserole   59
   Chicken Enchiladas   58
   Chicken Tacos   61
   Chicken Tostadas   57
   Fajita Marinade   66
   Fiesta Chicken   75
   Green Chile Burros   65
   Green Chile Chicken Burro   63
   Green Chile Sauce   54
   Mexican Lasagna   71
   Mexican Meatloaf   70
   Mexican Pizza   57
   Mexican Stuffed Peppers   68

Mexican Turkey Lasagna   72
Muy Pronto Salsa Roja   55
Pescado Veracruz   76
Red Chile Burros   64
Red Chile Sauce   55
Sloppy Jose's   75
Sonoran Enchiladas   60
Taco Shells   61
Tamale Pie   74
Turkey Tacos   62
meats
   beef, ground   56-58, 61
   beef tripe   32
   chicken
      breasts 23, 31, 37, 57-61, 63, 67, 75
   chuck roast   64-65, 69
   flank steak   67
   ham 26, 30, 43
   pork 51, 69, 74
   turkey 20, 23, 34-35, 40, 62, 68, 70,
      72, 74-75
Menudo   32
Meringues de Almendra   79
Meringues de Chocolate   79
Mexi-Macaroni   50
Mexican Casserole   49
Mexican Hot Chocolate   87
Mexican Lasagna   71
Mexican Meatloaf   70
Mexican Mocha   87
Mexican Pizza   57
Mexican Stuffed Peppers   68
Mexican Turkey Lasagna   72
Mission Burritos   26
Muy Pronto Salsa Roja   55
Nachos   19
Papas Colorado   47
Papas Verde   47
pasta 35, 50
Pastel Coctel de Fruta   82
Pastel de Piña   81
peas   35, 51
Pescado Veracruz   76
Pickled Potatoes   14
Pico de Gallo   19
Pinto Bean Soup   29

Potato Salad   38
Quick Salsa   10
Red Chile Burros   64
Red Chile Sauce   55
Refresco de Fresas   86
rice 30, 34, 40, 42, 45, 51-52, 68, 73, 78
Salsa Blanca   18
Salsa Picante   11
Salsa Verde   11
Salsas 9-11, 18
Sangria   86
Sangrita   85
Side Dishes
   Arroz de Mexico   51
   Black Beans & Corn   48
   Border Pasta   45
   Calabacitas   43
   Calabacitas con Jamón   43
   Chile Cornbread   46
   Chile Rice   45
   Chili Colorado   51
   Fiesta Hominy   52
   Frijoles   42
   Frijoles del Mar   48
   Green Chile Mashed Potatoes 44
   Hominy con Chile   46
   Lemon Rice   52
   Mexi-Macaroni   50
   Mexican Casserole   49
   Papas Colorado   47
   Papas Verde   47
   Spanish Rice   42
   Stuffed Baked Potatoes   49
   Sweet Potatoes   44
seafood
   red snapper 76
   shrimp   67, 76
   tuna   16, 48
Sloppy Jose's   75
Sonoran Enchiladas   61
Sopa de Fideo   35
Sopa de Papas   33
soups 46, 59, 63
Spanish Rice   42
Spicy Jicama Sticks   14
Spicy Medley   15

Soups & Salads
   Albondigas Soup   34
   Black Bean & Rice Soup   30
   Black Bean Salad   39
   Caldo de Pollo   31
   Chicken Taco Salad   37
   Corn Salad   39
   Ensalada de Pepiño   36
   Ensalada de Tres Frijoles   37
   Fiesta Salad   38
   Gazpacho   28
   Hearty Bean Soup   30
   Jicama Salad   36
   Menudo   32
   Pinto Bean Soup   29
   Potato Salad   38
   Sopa de Fideo   35
   Sopa de Papas   33
   Taco Soup   35
   Tortilla Soup   28
   Turkey and Rice Salad   40
squash
   summer 43
   zucchini   31, 43, 67
Stuffed Baked Potatoes   49
Stuffed Green Chiles   15
sweet potatoes   44
Sweet Potatoes   44
Sweet Tortilla Roll-ups   81
Taco Shells   60
Taco Soup   35
Tamale Pie   74
Tequila Sunrise   84
tomatillos 54
Torta de Chile Verde   25
Tortilla Roll-ups   16
Tortilla Soup   28
tortillas
   corn 8, 17, 24, 28, 56-61, 67, 71-72
   flour 8, 16-17, 23, 26, 57, 63-65, 67, 73-74,
      69, 81
Traditional Margarita   84
Tuna-stuffed Jalapeños   16
Turkey and Rice Salad   40
Turkey Tacos   62
Veggie Quesadillas   17

About the Authors

Shayne and Lee Fischer (she's Shayne and he's Lee) are natives of Arizona. Both grew up with an affinity for Mexican foods. Lee remembers the first restaurant he ever went to was a Mexican food restaurant. Shayne's early love for Mexican food was sparked by her mother's homemade tacos. In later years, Shayne spent many hours with a dear friend's grandmother, Nana Pacheco, watching her prepare authentic Mexican meals without benefit of any cookbooks.

Although not all of the recipes in this book are authentic Mexican recipes, they represent the Mexican style of cooking and fit into today's health-conscious lifestyles. As health and exercise enthusiasts, Shayne and Lee found it necessary to create these recipes so they could indulge more often in their favorite pastime, eating Mexican food!

Authors of two other cookbooks, *Vegi-Mex: Vegetarian Mexican Recipes* and *Wholly Frijoles: The Whole Bean Cook Book* (by Shayne), the Fischers live in Phoenix where they continue to pursue an active lifestyle which includes power walking, running, bicycling, hiking and eating Mexican food.

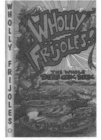

ORDER BLANK

GOLDEN WEST PUBLISHERS

☼ 4113 N. Longview Ave. • Phoenix, AZ 85014

www.goldenwestpublishers.com • **1-800-658-5830** • FAX 602-279-6901

Qty	Title	Price	Amount
	Best Barbecue Recipes	5.95	
	Chili-Lovers' Cook Book	5.95	
	Chip and Dip Lovers Cook Book	5.95	
	Cowboy Cartoon Cook Book	7.95	
	Gourmet Gringo Cook Book	14.95	
	Grand Canyon Cook Book	6.95	
	Kokopelli's Cook Book	9.95	
	Low Fat Mexican Recipes	6.95	
	Mexican Desserts & Drinks	6.95	
	New Mexico Cook Book	5.95	
	Quick-n-Easy Mexican Recipes	5.95	
	Real New Mexico Chile	6.95	
	Recipes for a Healthy Lifestyle	6.95	
	Salsa Lovers Cook Book	5.95	
	Take This Chile & Stuff It!	6.95	
	Tequila Cook Book	7.95	
	Tortilla Lovers Cook Book	6.95	
	Veggie Lovers Cook Book	6.95	
	Vegi-Mex: Vegetarian Mexican Recipes	6.95	
	Wholly Frijoles! The Whole Bean Cook Book	6.95	
Shipping & Handling Add ➠	U.S. & Canada / Other countries	$3.00 / $5.00	

☐ My Check or Money Order Enclosed $

☐ MasterCard ☐ VISA ($20 credit card minimum)

(Payable in U.S. funds)

Acct. No.   Exp. Date

Signature

Name   Telephone

Address

City/State/Zip **Call for a FREE catalog of all of our titles** Low Fat Mexican Recipes
05/01

This order blank may be photo-copied.